Iraq

Other Books of Related Interest:

Opposing Viewpoints Series

The Middle East

At Issue Series

What Role Should the U.S. Play in the Middle East?

Current Controversies Series

Darfur

"Congress shall make no law . . . abridging the freedom of speech, or of the press."

First Amendment to the U.S. Constitution

The basic foundation of our democracy is the First Amendment guarantee of freedom of expression. The Opposing Viewpoints Series is dedicated to the concept of this basic freedom and the idea that it is more important to practice it than to enshrine it.

OPPOSING
VIEWPOINTS®
SERIES

Iraq

David M. Haugen, Susan Musser, and Kacy Lovelace,
Book Editors

WITHDRAWN

GREENHAVEN PRESS
A part of Gale, Cengage Learning

GALE
CENGAGE Learning™

Detroit • New York • San Francisco • New Haven, Conn • Waterville, Maine • London

Christine Nasso, *Publisher*
Elizabeth Des Chenes, *Managing Editor*

© 2009 Greenhaven Press, a part of Gale, Cengage Learning.

Gale and Greenhaven Press are registered trademarks used herein under license.

For more information, contact:
Greenhaven Press
27500 Drake Rd.
Farmington Hills, MI 48331-3535
Or you can visit our Internet site at gale.cengage.com

For product information and technology assistance, contact us at

Gale Customer Support, 1-800-877-4253

For permission to use material from this text or product, submit all requests online at www.cengage.com/permissions

Further permissions questions can be emailed to permissionrequest@cengage.com

Articles in Greenhaven Press anthologies are often edited for length to meet page requirements. In addition, original titles of these works are changed to clearly present the main thesis and to explicitly indicate the author's opinion. Every effort is made to ensure that Greenhaven Press accurately reflects the original intent of the authors. Every effort has been made to trace the owners of copyrighted material.

Cover photograph reproduced by © Benjamin Cowy/Corbis.

LIBRARY OF CONGRESS CATALOGING-IN-PUBLICATION DATA

Iraq / David M. Haugen, Susan Musser, and Kacy Lovelace, book editors.
    p. cm. -- (Opposing viewpoints)
    Includes bibliographical references and index.
    ISBN 978-0-7377-4524-5 (hardcover)
    ISBN 978-0-7377-4525-2 (pbk.)
    1. Iraq--Politics and government--2003---Juvenile literature. 2. Iraq--Ethnic relations--Juvenile literature. 3. United States--Foreign relations--Iraq--Juvenile literature. 4. Iraq--Foreign relations--United States--Juvenile literature. 5. Iraq War, 2003---Juvenile literature. 6. War on Terrorism, 2001---Juvenile literature. 7. Terrorism--Prevention--Government policy--United States--Juvenile literature.
    I. Haugen, David M., 1969- II. Musser, Susan. III. Lovelace, Kacy.
    DS79.769.I725 2009
    956.7044'3--dc22
                                                                2008051446

Printed in the United States of America
1 2 3 4 5 6 7 13 12 11 10 09

Contents

Why Consider Opposing Viewpoints?

> *"The only way in which a human being can make some approach to knowing the whole of a subject is by hearing what can be said about it by persons of every variety of opinion and studying all modes in which it can be looked at by every character of mind. No wise man ever acquired his wisdom in any mode but this."*
>
> *John Stuart Mill*

In our media-intensive culture it is not difficult to find differing opinions. Thousands of newspapers and magazines and dozens of radio and television talk shows resound with differing points of view. The difficulty lies in deciding which opinion to agree with and which "experts" seem the most credible. The more inundated we become with differing opinions and claims, the more essential it is to hone critical reading and thinking skills to evaluate these ideas. Opposing Viewpoints books address this problem directly by presenting stimulating debates that can be used to enhance and teach these skills. The varied opinions contained in each book examine many different aspects of a single issue. While examining these conveniently edited opposing views, readers can develop critical thinking skills such as the ability to compare and contrast authors' credibility, facts, argumentation styles, use of persuasive techniques, and other stylistic tools. In short, the Opposing Viewpoints Series is an ideal way to attain the higher-level thinking and reading skills so essential in a culture of diverse and contradictory opinions.

In addition to providing a tool for critical thinking, Opposing Viewpoints books challenge readers to question their own strongly held opinions and assumptions. Most people form their opinions on the basis of upbringing, peer pressure, and personal, cultural, or professional bias. By reading carefully balanced opposing views, readers must directly confront new ideas as well as the opinions of those with whom they disagree. This is not to simplistically argue that everyone who reads opposing views will—or should—change his or her opinion. Instead, the series enhances readers' understanding of their own views by encouraging confrontation with opposing ideas. Careful examination of others' views can lead to the readers' understanding of the logical inconsistencies in their own opinions, perspective on why they hold an opinion, and the consideration of the possibility that their opinion requires further evaluation.

Evaluating Other Opinions

To ensure that this type of examination occurs, Opposing Viewpoints books present all types of opinions. Prominent spokespeople on different sides of each issue as well as well-known professionals from many disciplines challenge the reader. An additional goal of the series is to provide a forum for other, less known, or even unpopular viewpoints. The opinion of an ordinary person who has had to make the decision to cut off life support from a terminally ill relative, for example, may be just as valuable and provide just as much insight as a medical ethicist's professional opinion. The editors have two additional purposes in including these less known views. One, the editors encourage readers to respect others' opinions—even when not enhanced by professional credibility. It is only by reading or listening to and objectively evaluating others' ideas that one can determine whether they are worthy of consideration. Two, the inclusion of such viewpoints encourages the important critical thinking skill of objectively evaluating an author's credentials and bias. This evaluation will illuminate an author's reasons for taking a particular stance on an issue and will aid in readers' evaluation of the author's ideas.

It is our hope that these books will give readers a deeper understanding of the issues debated and an appreciation of the complexity of even seemingly simple issues when good and honest people disagree. This awareness is particularly important in a democratic society such as ours in which people enter into public debate to determine the common good. Those with whom one disagrees should not be regarded as enemies but rather as people whose views deserve careful examination and may shed light on one's own.

Thomas Jefferson once said that "difference of opinion leads to inquiry, and inquiry to truth." Jefferson, a broadly educated man, argued that "if a nation expects to be ignorant and free ... it expects what never was and never will be." As individuals and as a nation, it is imperative that we consider the opinions of others and examine them with skill and discernment. The Opposing Viewpoints Series is intended to help readers achieve this goal.

David L. Bender and Bruno Leone,
Founders

Introduction

> *"Mission accomplished? If the mission was to create conditions giving rise to sectarian violence, a growing insurgency, and all-out civil war, while dragging [the United States] to the brink of bankruptcy, then, yes, you might say that."*
>
> Justin Raimondo,
> May 2, 2005. www.antiwar.com.

On May 1, 2003, aboard the USS *Abraham Lincoln*, President George W. Bush declared an end to major combat operations in Iraq. It had been only eleven days since the United States and allied coalition forces had invaded Iraq to depose the despotic regime of Saddam Hussein and to destroy stockpiles of weapons of mass destruction (WMD) that Western leaders believed Hussein was hoarding. When Bush stood on the deck of the *Abraham Lincoln* in front of a banner that read "Mission Accomplished," coalition soldiers had yet to locate any WMD—indeed, they never found any such stockpiles in the ensuing occupation of Iraq—but they had destroyed the war-making capacity of the Iraqi army and freed the population from nearly a quarter of a century of oppressive rule.

Ironically, in the President's speech given that day in front of that banner, Bush stated, "Our mission continues.... The enemies of freedom are not idle, and neither are we.... The war on terror is not over, yet it is not endless. We do not know the day of final victory, but we have seen the turning of the tide." He insisted that the "liberation" of Iraq was "a crucial advance in the campaign against terror." Yet while the administration briefly reveled in the toppling of Saddam Hussein, critics of the war were doubtful that the end of the tyrant would bring true liberation to the Iraqi people. In September 2003, *Time* magazine ran a headline on its cover that blared "Mission Not Accomplished." Within its pages, *Time* reported that 170 U.S. soldiers had died in Iraq since the May speech, and two potential Iraqi leaders and a United Nations representative had been killed by terrorist acts. The magazine also noted increasing incidents of sabotage by insurgents as well as the rumblings of a populace that was initially pleased to see Hussein deposed but now was beginning to chafe at occupation. *Time* reporters quoted Ahmed Chalabi, an Iraqi exile favored by the Bush administration as a new leader among his people, confessing, "When the U.S. said we are not liberators, we are an occupation force, the views of people changed."

Over the next five years, insurgency in Iraq grew steadily, and today its various factions remain active and hostile. The primary resistance is from groups led by the Sunni Arab minority, some of which are tribes that were once loyal to Saddam Hussein. Most of these groups favor a strict Muslim state and despise a Western presence in Iraq. Their militancy has been compounded by Shiite Arab militias—some of whom are backed by Iran—that clash with Sunnis and coalition forces alike. In addition, there are foreign fighters and terrorists who have come to Iraq to seize the opportunity to strike at Western—primarily American—invaders and foment Arab discontent at U.S. involvement in the Middle East. The Web site of the PBS news show *Frontline* asserts that the various insurgent groups are hampered by their lack of cooperation and could never hope to defeat coalition units or Iraq's own governmental security forces. Instead, as *Frontline* contends, the insurgents aim may be to "make the country essentially ungovernable, and deny the population the security and basic needs expected by them from their newly elected government."

Frontline sees the democratic process as a potential victim of continued conflict in Iraq if the people feel threatened enough to sacrifice liberties for safety by backing warlords or strongmen to bring peace. Such an outcome would be disastrous to U.S. goals given that President Bush has made the establishment of Iraqi democracy a part of the American mission since 2003. Although Iraqi civilians have not embraced a return to oppression to end the insurgency, it is unclear whether the nation is any closer to democracy than it was before the coalition invasion.

Writing in the *Christian Science Monitor,* Lawrence E. Harrison asserts that democracy in Iraq "is vastly complicated by the longstanding hostility between the majority Shiite and the minority Sunni, and between those two Arab sects and the Iraqi Kurds." Indeed, despite the presence of a new U.S.-backed central government and the holding of elections in 2005 (which Sunnis claimed were unfair), many question whether Iraqi nationalism will foster unity. Several U.S. politicians and observers believe that Iraq should be partitioned into Sunni, Shiite, and Kurdish states—a resolution that many Kurds, the tribal people living mainly in mountainous northern Iraq, support. Advocates of partition expect that the best Iraq can hope for is a weak federalist government with power shifted mainly to the separate states. Several Iraqis—including many in the newly elected government—have rejected partition and insist that Iraqi nationalism is a strong bond that will keep the various ethnic and religious groups together.

Some organizations such as USAID, the United States Agency for International Development, contend that civic participation is flourishing at the local and district levels where, according to one report, "more than 80 percent of Iraq's adult population has been engaged—either directly or indirectly—in democracy or governance." And Eric Davis, writing for the United Nations Institute for Peace, maintains that "a truly democratic society is characterized by a high level of political participation and an organized citizenry." Davis sees many facets of Iraqi society as prerequisites for effective democracy, including an emphasis on education, a respect for legal traditions, and a history of intellectual and cultural tolerance.

Davis and others hope that the current insurgency will not shake the confidence of the Iraqi people or tempt America to trade democracy-building for pacification.

The small-scale democratic advances, however, have not translated across sectarian lines and a unity of the Sunnis, Shiites, and Kurds has not resulted from the 2005 elections. Critics suggest the government of Prime Minister Nouri al-Maliki has done little to bridge gaps. CNN reported in 2007 that seventeen of the thirty-five cabinet members in the new Iraqi government either boycott or fail to attend meetings. It also confirmed that the government is still unable to supply all of Iraq's people with running water or electricity. The cable network even claimed that high-ranking U.S. military commanders in Iraq have suggested in private that the whole Iraqi government should be replaced with "a stable, secure, but not necessarily democratic entity."

In *Opposing Viewpoints: Iraq*, various politicians, commentators, journalists, and scholars examine U.S. endeavors to end insurgency and bring democracy to Iraq. In chapters entitled How Capable Is the New Iraqi Regime? Should Iraq Be Partitioned Into Ethnic States? What Should U.S. Policy Be Toward a Post-War Iraq? and How Has War in Iraq Affected Terrorism? these authors and speechmakers debate American and Iraqi efforts to rebuild Iraq and to meet the post-war goals established by President Bush. The majority agrees that the mission in Iraq is far from accomplished, but there is still no consensus on whether the nation is headed for democracy, civil war, or dissolution. What is certain is that the future of Iraq will depend as much upon U.S. interests as it does upon the perseverance of the free people of Iraq to write their own history.

OPPOSING
VIEWPOINTS®
SERIES

CHAPTER 1

How Capable Is the New Iraqi Regime?

Chapter Preface

Recent public opinion surveys in Iraq have shown that the greatest concern facing Iraqi citizens is criminal violence and not the fear of sectarian conflict or insurgency. The main reason for this concern is the Iraqi National Police Force, which according to a recent assessment by the State Department, is responsible for countless abuses of power. But calls to disband the police force have been denied by senior U.S. military personnel in Iraq who claim that breaking up the force would endanger security.

The list of accusations against the Iraqi National Police is vast. Officers have been accused of keeping secret prisons and raping female prisoners, and as Human Rights Watch noted during extensive interviews with Iraqi prisoners, "torture and ill-treatment under interrogation are routine." The police force is also accused of accepting bribes to release terrorist suspects, participating in insurgent bombings, and assassinating officers in its own ranks.

Ayad Allawi, Iraq's first prime minister after the fall of Suddam Hussein's regime, believes that human rights violations in Iraq are equal in number if not greater than those suffered under Hussein's despotic rule. Part of this is due to the fact that Iraq's police have never been accustomed to the duties of law enforcement. Under Hussein's rule, spy networks and fear of the state's power kept Iraq's streets relatively clear of violence. The Iraqi National Police were on the lowest rung of the security ladder, never patrolling and only called upon when an arrest was necessary. When the U.S. military created the new Iraqi National Police, officers filled a more prominent role, but their lack of proper training and procedural methods meant that many relied on intimidation to break witnesses and suspects. In addition, many police units—especially in central and southern Iraq—were quickly infiltrated by members of Shiite militias who had their own agendas to wipe out Sunni Arab rivals. According to a 2005 report by the Council of Foreign Relations, Sunni organizations put together a list "alleging hundreds of extrajudicial killings, disappearances, illegal raids, and instances of torture of Sunnis by individuals linked to Shiite militias."

With the violence that plagues the nation appearing within the very forces that are supposed to quell that violence, many are skeptical that the majority of police units are anything but another faction in what amounts to a civil war. Major Jerry Burke, an American who served for two years as a senior advisor on police affairs to the Iraqi Ministry of the Interior, argues succinctly, "The National Police is not salvageable. It should be disbanded and many of its members should be prosecuted for criminal human rights violations, war crimes, and death squad activities."

However, not everyone has taken such a grim view of police conduct. After all, thousands of Iraqi police have lost their lives in the line of duty, and many dedicated men and women officers are hoping to bring peace to their communities. Furthermore, as Michael J. Totten notes in the following chapter, Kurdish police forces in northern Iraq are not often embroiled in sectarian in-fighting and appear to be operating quite effectively. Totten's viewpoint and others in this chapter suggest that the stability and capability of the new Iraqi regime may rest on how well the government and law enforcement can bring the people of Iraq together.

> "The unity government has strong leaders that will represent all of the Iraqi people."

Iraq Has a Capable New Government

George W. Bush

George W. Bush was the forty-third president of the United States. He presided over the 2003 invasion of Iraq and its ongoing occupation. In the following viewpoint, Bush speaks of the creation of the unity government in Iraq in May 2006—the first democratically elected government to hold office after the downfall of the despotic Iraqi leader Saddam Hussein. The president applauds the new prime minister of Iraq, Nouri al-Maliki, and his colleagues for promoting ethnic and religious diversity in the unity government and for their commitment to democracy, justice, and human rights for all Iraqi people. With such a capable new government, Bush expects that the United States will revert to a supporting role in ensuring future success in Iraq's push toward stability and peace.

As you read, consider the following questions:

1. As Bush explains, who is Jalal Talabani?

George W. Bush, "President George W. Bush's Address: Iraq's National Unity Government," U.S. Department of State, May 22, 2006. U.S. Department of State, Washington, DC.

2. According to Bush, what promises did Prime Minister Maliki make when laying out his initial plan for a new Iraq?

3. In Bush's view, what changed for terrorists in Iraq over the weekend of May 20–21, 2006?

We face challenges at home and we face challenges abroad. So I've come to talk to you about an historic event that took place halfway around the world this weekend. This Saturday [May 20, 2006] in Baghdad, the new Prime Minister of Iraq [Nouri al-Maliki] announced a national unity government. This is a free government under a democratic constitution, and its formation marks a victory for the cause of freedom in the Middle East.

In three elections [in 2005], millions of Iraqis cast their ballot in defiance of the terrorists. And now they have a government of their own choosing under a constitution that they drafted and they approved. As this new unity government takes office, it carries with it the hopes of the Iraqi nation, and the aspirations of freedom-loving people across a troubled region.

The unity government has strong leaders that will represent all of the Iraqi people. I called them this weekend to congratulate them. I thanked them for being courageous and strong and standing for the belief that liberty will help transform their troubled nation.

The new government is led by Prime Minister Maliki. He's a Shia. He's an Iraqi patriot who for years was part of the resistance to Saddam Hussein. He's shown courage and wisdom by surrounding himself with strong leaders who are committed to serving all the people. Prime Minister Maliki said this weekend, "Just as we did away with the tyrant and the days of oppression and despotism, we will do away with terrorism and sabotage, backwardness, poverty, and ignorance." The

Iraqi people are blessed to have a leader like Prime Minister Maliki, and I'm proud to call him, ally and friend.

Iraq's new government has another strong leader in its President, President [Jalal] Talabani. He's a Kurd who distinguished himself by his service in the transitional government and in his long fight against Saddam Hussein. He's proved that he's not afraid to take the lead. He's made clear that a democratic Iraq must reject sectarian violence as strongly as it rejects terrorism. He says, "It's our duty, all of us, to work hand-in-hand to protect our people and to support Iraqi unity."

Iraq's new government has another able leader in Speaker [Mahmoud al-] Mashhadani. He'll preside over Iraq's new Council of Representatives. The Speaker is a Sunni who originally opposed America's presence in Iraq. He rejects the use of violence for political ends. And by agreeing to serve in a prominent role in this new unity government, he's demonstrating leadership and courage.

It was said to me that he wouldn't have taken my phone call a year ago. He's now taken it twice. He says Iraq's new leaders must govern by common vision. This common vision is critical to the new government's success.

Working to Heal Divisions

Although Iraq's new leaders come from many different ethnic and religious communities, they've made clear they will govern as Iraqis. They know that the strategy of the terrorists and the insurgents is to divide Iraq along sectarian lines. And the only way the enemy will be defeated is if they stand and act as one.

The government is still a work in progress, and overcoming long-standing divisions will take time. Iraq's new leaders know they have a great deal of work ahead to broaden the base of their government and to unite the people. They also understand that representing all Iraqis and not just narrow sectarian interests, they will be able to make a decisive break with the past and make a future of progress and opportunity for all their people a reality. The unity government must now seize its moment and pursue a common agenda for the future.

This weekend [May 20–21, 2006], Prime Minister Maliki laid out his plan for a new Iraq. He promised to work for a sovereign Iraq that will assume responsibility for the security of its people. He committed himself to a free Iraq that will uphold international standards of human rights and respect the role of women in Iraqi society. He pledged to work for a prosperous Iraq that welcomes foreign investments and accelerates reconstruction and lays the foundations for economic growth and opportunity. He declared he would lead a transparent Iraq, where government is open and accountable, and corruption is not tolerated. And he vowed to work for a peaceful Iraq that is the enemy of terror, a friend to its neighbors, and a reliable partner in the community of nations.

The Prime Minister promised that he will soon fill the remaining positions in his government, and announced the details of his plans to build his new country, his new Iraq. As his government moves forward, it can draw on many strengths of the Iraqi nation. Iraqis are among the most highly educated and skilled people in the Middle East. They have abundant natural resources, including fertile soil, abundant water, and large reserves of oil. And they're rich in cultural and historical and religious sites that one day could draw millions of tourists and pilgrims from across the world. Iraq's new leaders understand that so long as they remain united there is no limit to the potential of their country.

America's Support for the New Government

The unity government opens a new chapter in the relationship between the United States and Iraq. The new Iraqi government does not change America's objectives or our commitment, but it will change how we achieve those objectives and

Nouri al-Maliki Discusses Iraq's Progress

Spiegel: In your opinion, which factor has contributed most to bringing calm to the situation in the country?

Maliki: There are many factors, but I see them in the following order. First, there is the political rapprochement we have managed to achieve in central Iraq. This has enabled us, above all, to pull the plug on al-Qaida. Second, there is the progress being made by our security forces. Third, there is the deep sense of abhorrence with which the population has reacted to the atrocities of al-Qaida and the militias. Finally, of course, there is the economic recovery. . . .

Spiegel: How do you cope with [the dangers of your job]?

Maliki: I lead a very simple life—one that is shaped by external forces, which is apparently what fate has determined for us Iraqis. In that regard, the past few decades of dictatorship have not changed all that much. What keeps me going? The constant exertion of my job—and the successes we are now having. It means a lot to me to see how much closer we are today to a democratic Iraq, one that respects human rights, than we were only a few months ago.

Mathias Müller von Blumencron and Bernard Zand,
July 19, 2008. www.spiegel.de.

how we honor our commitment. And the new Iraqi government—as the new Iraqi government grows in confidence and capability, America will play an increasingly supporting role. To take advantage of this moment of opportunity, the United States and our coalition partners will work with the new Iraqi government to adjust our methods and strengthen our mutual efforts to achieve victory over our common enemies.

At my direction, the Secretaries of State and Defense recently traveled to Baghdad to meet with the Prime Minister and other leaders. And now the new government has been formed, I've instructed those Secretaries to engage Iraq's new leaders as they assess their needs and capabilities, so we will be in the best position to help them succeed. Iraqis are determined to chart their own future. And now they have the leadership to do it. And this unity government deserves American support, and they will have it.

Our nation has been through three difficult years in Iraq. And the way forward will bring more days of challenge and loss. The progress we've made has been hard-fought, and it's been incremental. There have been setbacks and missteps—like Abu Ghraib—that were felt immediately and have been difficult to overcome. Yet we have now reached a turning point in the struggle between freedom and terror.

Iraq Is Determined to Fight Terrorism

Two years ago, al Qaeda's leader in Iraq wrote a letter that said, "democracy is coming," and this would mean "suffocation" for al Qaeda and its allies. The terrorists fought this moment with all their hateful power—with suicide attacks, and beheadings, and roadside bombs—and now the day they feared has arrived. And with it has come a moment of great clarity: The terrorists can kill the innocent, but they cannot stop the advance of freedom.

The terrorists did not lay down their arms after three elections in Iraq, and they will continue to fight this new government. And we can expect the violence to continue, but something fundamental changed this weekend. The terrorists are now fighting a free and constitutional government. They're at war with the people of Iraq. And the Iraqi people are determined to defeat this enemy, and so are Iraq's new leaders, and so is the United States of America.

The path to freedom is always one of struggle and sacrifice. And in Iraq, our brave men and women in uniform have accepted the struggle and have made the sacrifice. This moment would not be possible without their courage. The United States of America is safer because of their success, and our nation will always be grateful to their service.

For most Iraqis, a free, democratic and constitutional government will be a new experience. And for the people across the broader Middle East, a free Iraq will be an inspiration. Iraqis have done more than form a government; they have proved that the desire for liberty in the heart of the Middle East is for real. They've shown diverse people can come together and work out their differences and find a way forward. And they've demonstrated that democracy is the hope of the Middle East and the destiny of all mankind.

The triumph of liberty in Iraq is part of a long and familiar story. The great biographer of American democracy, Alexis de Tocqueville, wrote: "Freedom is ordinarily born in the midst of storms. It is established painfully among civil discords, and only when it is old can one know its benefits." Years from now people will look back on the formation of a unity government in Iraq as a decisive moment in the story of liberty, a moment when freedom gained a firm foothold in the Middle East, and the forces of terror began their long retreat.

| *"Does anyone imagine that [Prime Min-
ister] Maliki enjoys the confidence of
the majority of Iraqis?"*

Iraq Has a Weak New Government

Charles Krauthammer

*In the viewpoint that follows, Charles Krauthammer asserts that
the new unity government of Iraq is a sham. In his view, the
Shiite-dominated government does not represent the will of the
different religious and ethnic peoples of Iraq, and he claims that
Prime Minister Nouri al-Maliki is indecisive and lacks the ability to forge the necessary compromises to bring the diverse Iraqi
factions together. Charles Krauthammer is a syndicated columnist for the* Washington Post. *He is also a political commentator
for Fox News.*

As you read, consider the following questions:

1. According to Krauthammer, what action taken by General David Petraeus was upsetting to the Maliki government?
2. What controversial statement did Prime Minister Maliki
   make in response to parliamentary calls to bring down
   his government?

Charles Krauthammer, "Weak and Unreliable: The Maliki Problem," *National Review
Online*, August 31, 2007. Reproduced by permission.

3. As Krauthammer explains, how are Iraqi members of parliament chosen under the current governing system?

The government of Iraqi Prime Minister Nouri al-Maliki has had more than 15 months to try to pacify the Sunni insurgency by offering national accords on oil-sharing, provincial elections and de-Baathification [the removal of the remnant of Saddam Hussein's Baath Party that formerly ruled Iraq]. It has done none of these. Instead, Gen. David Petraeus [commander of the multinational military force in Iraq] has pacified a considerable number of Sunni tribes with grants of local autonomy, guns, and U.S. support in jointly fighting al-Qaeda.

Petraeus's strategy is not very pretty. It carries risk. But it has been effective.

The Shiite-dominated government in Baghdad, however, is not happy with Petraeus's actions. One top Maliki aide complained that it will leave Iraq "an armed society and militias."

What does he think Iraq is now? Except that many Sunni militias that were once shooting at Americans are now shooting at al-Qaeda.

The Rift Between Washington and Baghdad

The nature of the war is changing. In July [2007], 73 percent of the attacks that caused U.S. casualties in Baghdad were from Shiite militants, not Sunnis. Maliki is no fool. As more Sunni tribes are pacified, he can see the final military chapter of this war coming into focus: the considerable power of the American military machine slowly turning its face—and its guns—on Shiite extremists.

Of the many mistakes committed in Iraq, perhaps the most serious was to have failed to destroy Moqtada al-Sadr and the remains of his ragged [Mahdi] army when we had him cornered and defeated in Najaf in 2004. As a consequence,

we have to face him once again. The troop surge has already begun deadly and significant raids into Mahdi strongholds in Baghdad.

Sadr is hurting. On Wednesday [August 29, 2007], after many were killed in Shiite-on-Shiite fighting in Karbala, he called for a six-month moratorium on all military operations in order to permit him to "rehabilitate" his increasingly disorganized forces.

At the same time, however, Maliki is denouncing us for overkill in our raids on Shiite areas. The rift between Washington and Baghdad is opening. It will only widen as long as Maliki is in power.

Indecisive Leadership

Now, Maliki is no friend of Sadr or Iran. He knows that if they ultimately prevail, they will swallow him whole. But Maliki is too weak temperamentally and politically to make the decisive move in the other direction—toward Sunni and Shiite moderates—in order to make the necessary national compromises.

So he hedges his bets. He visits Iran and, then, while on a Syrian visit, responds to calls for the Iraqi parliament to bring his government down by saying, "Those who make such statements are bothered by our visit to Syria," and warning darkly that Iraq "can find friends elsewhere."

Maliki is not just weak but unreliable. Time is short. We should have long ago—say, when [National Security Advisor] Stephen Hadley wrote his leaked memo last November [2006] about Maliki's failure—begun working to have this dysfunctional government replaced.

Even the French foreign minister, upon returning from a recent fence-mending trip to Iraq, called for Maliki's replacement. (One can discount his later apology as pro forma.) Such suggestions are often denounced as hypocritical and contrary to democracy. Nonsense. In a parliamentary system, a government serves only if it continues to command confidence.

Does anyone imagine that Maliki enjoys the confidence of the majority of Iraqis? If he does not, parliament, representing the people, has the perfect right to vote no confidence and bring down the government.

New, Democratic Elections Are Needed

And then? Rather than seek a new coalition as a shaky substitute, the better alternative is new elections. And this time we must not repeat the mistake of election by party list, a system almost designed to produce warlord leadership and unstable coalitions.

Sen. Lindsey Graham [of South Carolina], returning from two weeks of reserve duty in Iraq, noted that the August [2007] parliamentary recess was beneficial because it allowed the members to hear from angry hometown citizens demanding political compromise and peace. But the problem with the current system is that Iraqi MPs [members of parliament] are not elected by their hometown citizens. They are chosen by party bosses.

A sample of the countries that have chosen this absurd form of democracy—Italy, Israel and Weimar Germany—gives you an idea of the balkanized unstable politics party-list systems inevitably produce. With a constituency system—members elected by a real geographic entity—the Anbar sheiks would be sitting in parliament negotiating on behalf of Sunnis, rather than members of a faux-national Sunni party that represents very little.

New elections are not a panacea [remedy]. They will take long to organize—which is why we should have been working toward this months ago. But the reconciliation from below that is actually happening in the provinces could—and logically should—be making national reconciliation possible in Baghdad. We can't sit around forever waiting for Maliki.

> *"The reputation of the police force now lies in tatters, amid accusations of human-rights violations and other police abuses."*

Iraqi Police Forces Are Unreliable

Kevin Whitelaw

In the following viewpoint, Kevin Whitelaw describes a dismal picture of the Iraqi police forces that have been assembled to secure Baghdad and fight insurgent militias. Whitelaw states that the Iraqi police are poorly led, poorly trained, and are consistently outgunned by their enemies. According to Whitelaw, some police units have become factionalized, purging themselves and the neighborhoods they are meant to protect of political and religious opponents. In Whitelaw's view, these rogue units have simply become another warring party let loose on the streets of the capital. Kevin Whitelaw covers national security and foreign affairs for U.S. News & World Report.

As you read, consider the following questions:

1. How much money was set aside to train Iraqi police, according to Whitelaw?

Kevin Whitelaw, "Baghdad Blues: For Three Years, the U.S. Has Tried to Build Iraq's Police Force. Why It's Still a Mess," *U.S. News & World Report*, April 10, 2006. Reprinted with permission.

2. What changes did Falah al-Naqib bring to the Iraqi police and commando projects?

3. What did U.S. forces uncover during a raid on an Iraqi Interior Ministry bunker in November 2005?

Inside a low-slung bunker in a quiet residential neighborhood in Baghdad, Falah al-Naqib was holding court in his temporary office. It was July 2004, and Iraq's new interior minister was briefing a team of U.S. civilian advisers on his plan to jump-start Iraq's moribund police force. A former Sunni opposition leader, Naqib wanted to bring back intact Iraqi Army units, which mirrored Iraq's ethnic and sectarian makeup, to form a new police commando force that could tackle an alarming spike in violence.

Within a few weeks, the first recruits were training, even though they lacked uniforms—and in some cases, shoes. When Matt Sherman, a U.S. adviser, first saw the unit, he was impressed by its tight discipline and high morale. The commandos soon received support from the U.S. military and gained respect from other Iraqis after battling insurgents in several cities. "They literally were the most effective [Iraqi] fighting force," says Sherman. "What was great about it was that the Iraqis were doing it on their own."

Renegade Police

The glow has long since faded. Today, the bunker where this brief success story was conceived is better known as the site of an illegal detention center apparently run by a renegade force within the Interior Ministry. The reputation of the police force now lies in tatters, amid accusations of human-rights violations and other police abuses. And many Sunnis have come to distrust the commandos, now called the National Police, while the ministry is widely believed by Iraqis to be riddled with hard-line Shiite militias that have free rein to pursue their own, often violent, agendas. Suspicion has only grown in the past two weeks after a string of deadly raids on Baghdad businesses by gunmen dressed in Iraqi commando uniforms.

The need for a reliable and integrated police force has never been greater. Iraq is facing a dangerous surge of sectarian violence with insurgents scheming to provoke a full-scale civil war. But these days, the embattled Interior Ministry has become a symbol of the [George W.] Bush administration's inability to establish basic security in central Iraq. There were some early successes, such as the commandos, but broader progress has been undone by the vagaries of Iraq's emerging political scene and the ever rising violence. The failures were compounded by intense squabbles and profound disconnects inside the U.S. government effort. U.S. military officials point to signs of progress: Police are better able to hold their ground against insurgent attacks, and the ministry has disbanded some outlaw units in recent months. But other U.S. officials insist that the ministry urgently needs to be depoliticized to help stave off a civil war. "I think it's one of our biggest problems," says a senior U.S. official.

Rebuilding was always going to be difficult, given Iraq's recent history of oppression. But, as with most of the reconstruction effort, U.S. officials did very little pre-invasion planning for rebuilding the crucial Interior Ministry, which oversees the police nationwide as well as the border and customs forces. When Steve Casteel arrived in Baghdad in the fall of 2003 to be the ministry's senior adviser, he had no time for illusions. On his first morning, the 32-year veteran of the Drug Enforcement Administration pulled up at the Al Rashid Hotel, which was to be his home, to watch smoke billowing from the hulking structure, which had just been rocketed by insurgents. The next day, suicide bombers hit four Baghdad police stations, killing eight officers. And on the third day, an aide warned that the ministry had somehow misplaced $72 million. (The money was located days later.) "So by the third day, I was asking, 'Is Iraq like this every day?'" he says.

Rebuilding the Police Force

In those early days, under the U.S.-led Coalition Provisional Authority [CPA], U.S. officials largely operated inside the confines of the Green Zone [the part of Baghdad with the greatest international presence], cut off from many Iraqis. Casteel had a mission—to rebuild the police—and a big budget, but few aides. "It was my first assignment in government where money wasn't the problem," says Casteel, who had served Latin America. "[Yet] I only had 19 people on my staff."

The pace was frenetic, as aides drafted a raft of plans—many idealistic, some even fanciful—usually with little Iraqi input. One CPA staffer who came from the Department of Homeland Security kept peddling a color-coded threat alert system for Iraq, similar to the much-ridiculed U.S. system. Other officials actually bought a $250 million digital radio system, only to have it rejected by Iraqis as too complicated and too costly—at $20 million a year—to operate.

Meanwhile, a host of serious problems loomed—the ragged, poorly trained police force was increasingly outgunned by the growing insurgency. Casteel wanted to build a national police force, but many CPA officials were leery of re-creating powerful, centralized security bodies. The staff advising the Interior Ministry was one of the larger U.S. teams, but Casteel's squad never got close to the 120 people he needed in order to manage the sprawling ministry. He topped out near 60, with high turnover, and many advisers lacked law enforcement expertise.

The immediate imperative was to train and deploy as many police officers as possible. "If you have overwhelming presence on the streets, you create a deterrent and you unleash intelligence," says Robert Charles, who ran the State Department's law enforcement bureau at the time. The plan, based on U.S.

work in Kosovo [in the former Yugoslavia] was an eight-week basic training course, followed by on-the-job mentoring by western police officers.

Frustrated by the slow pace of training, the Pentagon took over the program. (What's more, most of Casteel's staff erroneously were sent pink slips and instructions to leave Iraq within three days.) There was another wrinkle as a bitter bureaucratic battle raged for several months over a large chunk of the $800 million training effort. Some in Washington, like Charles, were impatient to get foreign police mentors deployed and blamed other U.S. officials for not helping. In Iraq, meanwhile, Casteel saw few mentors arriving and concluded that the violence would prevent sending them outside the capital. Instead, he wanted to move $950 million to pay for advanced training for skills like criminal investigation and bomb disposal. Eventually, the Baghdad team won the battle, but the delay was costly. "There was an appalling lack of a sense of urgency on the part of this administration to make sure that we were coherent at the execution level," says Paul Eaton, the retired major general who was in charge of training the Iraqi military and police at the time.

Naqib Takes Over

Meanwhile, the CPA was handing over authority to a temporary Iraqi government and a new U.S. Embassy. But some things were lost in the transition. The CPA wanted to create a commission to manage the integration of Iraq's sectarian militias, like the Shiite Badr Corps and the Kurdish peshmerga, into the security forces. The idea was to allow fighters to enlist as individuals and disavow loyalty to the militia, which some officials thought far-fetched. Either way, neither the new Iraqi government nor the new embassy staff was interested in the commission, which was not funded and eventually disappeared. This left the militia problem waiting to re-emerge.

The change of government also brought a macho new interior minister, Naqib, known for favoring fancy suits, dark sunglasses, and cigars. Not content to remain in the Green Zone, Naqib regularly traveled the country in a massive armored convoy. After a bloody U.S. offensive in Fallujah, the heart of the insurgency, he insisted on walking the streets there. "Of course, it was dangerous, but what should we do?" says Naqib. "Either you're a leader, or you're not." (It was dangerous for the Americans, too. Officials foiled a plot by the minister's tea server to poison Naqib and Casteel.)

As minister, Naqib worked quickly to build up his commando project. He fired corrupt or incompetent officers and raised the salaries of those who remained. "We had to clean them out," he says. He also brought back many Sunnis who had been pushed out because of their ties to Saddam Hussein's regime. There were hiccups: The police forces in Fallujah and Mosul collapsed after insurgent assaults in 2004. When Naqib took office, the Baghdad police force had only 8,000 officers and 4,000 AK-47s [assault rifles].

Lacking Leadership and Control

Naqib accepted the U.S. target of 135,000 officers nationwide, setting off a scramble for new recruits. The U.S. military, in recruiting and training the police, operated largely independently of Casteel's team. Soon, thousands of Iraqis were going through eight-week courses at police academies in Iraq and Jordan. "There was a constant drive to focus on the numbers, as if success was determined only by the numbers trained," says Sherman. "But you need leaders—that's what's been lacking with the police force."

The ministry was also lacking the capacity to absorb the recruits. Already, salaries were frequently going unpaid, sparking protests and desertions. Now, it was taking months to place the newly trained officers in police stations. The disconnect between the training side and the ministry

Corrupt and Dangerous Police Units

The Americans had to reconstitute the police [in 2006] since officers fled in droves after the invasion, ahead of gangs of looters. But the rush to replenish the ranks lacked proper controls, American, British and Iraqi officials said, and in the process political loyalists of the newly powerful were made officers, and there were reports of police jobs sold for kickbacks of $100.

In recent background checks, police investigators found more than 5,000 police officers with arrest records for crimes that included attacks on American troops, American officials said.

When the rebuilt skeletal force became a target of the rapidly spreading insurgency, Americans turned to heavily armed police commando units that had been assembled by the Iraqis. They added firepower, but at a price.

An Iraqi official who helped create the special units said he warned Defense Secretary Donald H. Rumsfeld that they could become a weapon in Iraq's sectarian strife, much as Mr. Hussein's police had repressed the Shiite majority. Now, after a year in which a Shiite interior minister controlled the police, some special units stand accused by many Sunnis of operating as Shiite-dominated death squads.

Michael Moss, New York Times, May 22, 2006.

was severe enough that neither side could even track where tens of thousands of trainees ended up.

The small civilian team was just struggling to keep up with the numbers. "Nobody focused on building institutional capacity for the police, just on training entry-level police," says one U.S. official currently involved in the program. "Instead, it became a cult based on the minister's personality." There was also a concern about the vetting process run by the U.S. military with little Iraqi input. Some U.S. officials believe that militia members—and even insurgents—were able to slip through the cracks.

Naqib's term in office lasted less than a year. There was an election in January 2005, but in the more than three months it took to hash out a new government, the ministry lost control over many local police forces. Provincial councils formed more quickly and usually installed their own local police chiefs. "New police chiefs, especially in the south, would fire the police forces and put militias in their place," says Casteel.

The current interior minister, Bayan Jabr, finally took office in late April 2005. He is a senior leader in the influential Shiite religious party Supreme Council for Islamic Revolution in Iraq [SCIRI], which had bargained hard to run the ministry. The commandos were viewed as a prize, because they were a national force that could operate independently—unlike Army units, which had to work closely with U.S. forces. SCIRI officials came into office convinced that Naqib, in recruiting for his commando unit, had allowed former Baath Party officials and some insurgent elements to return.

Iraqis Left on Their Own

U.S. officials, meanwhile, worried that Jabr would absorb into the police elements of the Badr Corps, the military wing of SCIRI. "With the militias, we tried to take them as individuals, not as a unit," says Casteel. "That changed with this government." Naqib now accuses his successor, Jabr, of purging some of his best units because they had many Sunnis. "They brought in new people," he says, who were mostly Shiites. U.S. military officials acknowledge that some local police forces remain infiltrated by militias but say that Jabr does not tolerate the practice. A Baghdad police captain in an investigations office, however, says that Sunnis in the force have been discriminated against and that Badr Corps fighters have been brought into the ministry with broad authority. "I see units go out on patrol in the night without any orders from anyone or even a court order signed by a judge," the captain, a Sunni, says. "We have our own civil war in the Ministry of Interior."

Casteel left Iraq soon after the transition. Gradually, the civilian advising team, which had kept offices inside the Interior Ministry, was ordered by the State Department to withdraw to the embassy. Jabr also wanted a more hands-off approach. "We were really kind of blocked out of a lot of things," says Sherman, who left in December.

Quickly, it became difficult for U.S. officials to track developments. They would receive reports of Shiite units carrying out unilateral operations in Sunni areas. Rumors of "death squads" spread as more and more bodies of men who had been killed execution-style began turning up on Iraqi streets. U.S. officials could rarely determine when the ministry was involved—and when it wasn't. Naqib is very critical of Jabr's management, saying the ministry is looking more like groups of militias. "Either they're for the people or against the people," he says. "What's happening now, it's against the people, like we had in Saddam's time."

Reports of Torture and Death Squads

Indeed, the gist of the rumors seemed to be confirmed in November [2005] when U.S. forces raided the Interior Ministry bunker where the commandos had been originally conceived. The search uncovered a secret detention area that held nearly 170 prisoners, some of whom had been starved or beaten. U.S. officials were furious. A U.S. aide walked into Jabr's office the following morning carrying a box with several whips sticking out—a collection of alleged torture implements found at the bunker. An Iraqi investigation is still pending.

Jabr would later insist the reports of tortured prisoners were exaggerated, calling them a ploy to sway voters in the December election for the first government under Iraq's new Constitution. He has publicly denied tolerating militias or death squads inside the ministry, which declined to comment for this story.

The U.S. military, meanwhile, had grown so concerned about the faltering police and hollow bureaucracy that it took over the ministry advising role in October [2005]. Today [April 2006], U.S. officials are deeply divided over Jabr's performance. Some, who were critical early, now praise him. "We believed a lot of the intelligence that said he was the reason for the sectarian divide in the ministry," says Maj. Gen. Joseph Peterson, the ministry's current senior adviser. "I've tested him, and he has always been national, not sectarian, in his decisions." He notes that Jabr has fired special police commanders and disbanded a rogue, predominantly Shiite, internal affairs unit. But others blame him for the ministry's lack of accountability. "He's either incompetent and not able to exercise control, or he is compliant," says a senior U.S. official.

Peterson says that after two years of focus on the quantity of police, he is trying to "put a little more quality into the force." Specifically, he plans to embed some 200 teams of U.S. military and civilian police mentors into local police stations and fully staff posts in the 10 most contested cities by June [2006].

Little Has Changed in Baghdad

Casteel, who now works for Vance, a security consulting firm, recently returned for a visit and met with a few former ministry officials in Jordan who say there are some 400 Sunnis ousted from the ministry in Jordan alone. "The more you politicize the ministry, the more likely a civil war will happen because you end up with units that are not loyal to the central government," says Casteel.

These days in Baghdad, dozens of new corpses continue to turn up on the streets each week, many of them blindfolded with their hands bound. The Mahdi Army, the militia headed by firebrand Shiite cleric Moqtada al-Sadr, and the Badr Corps continue to operate freely. And the talks to form a new government, which would name the next interior minister, have stretched out for more than three months. In the tumultuous nation, police remain on the front lines—some 2,700 have been killed in the past 18 months.

> *"Everyone who said anything about [the Iraqi police in Ramadi] insists they are dedicated and reliable."*

Iraqi Police Forces Are Becoming More Reliable

Michael J. Totten

In the following viewpoint, Michael J. Totten writes of his experiences traveling in Iraq and meeting with Iraqi police forces. Totten acknowledges that some police units in Iraq are known for corruption and abuses of power, but says that those he lived with in Ramadi showed a dedication to duty that seemed exemplary for an organization that had to battle insurgents as well as provide common law enforcement. Michael J. Totten is an independent journalist who covers Middle Eastern affairs. His work has appeared in a variety of publications including the New York Times *and the* Wall Street Journal.

As you read, consider the following questions:

1. Why was Totten impressed by the relative cleanliness of the Al Majed police station?
2. As Totten relates, what type of police work did Colonel Rahman say his men were engaged in now that the major fighting in the region has ended?

Michael J. Totten, "The Best Police Force in Iraq," *Michael J. Totten's Middle East Journal*, October 8, 2007. Reproduced by permission.

3. Who are the men who wear orange bands, according to Totten?

In late July [2007] when I visited a police station in the town of Mushadah just north of Baghdad I worried that Iraq was doomed to become the next Gaza. As many as half the police officers, according to most of the American Military Police who worked as their trainers, were Al Qaeda sympathizers or agents. The rest were corrupt lazy cowards, according to every American I talked to but one. No one tried to spin Mushadah into a success story. By itself this doesn't mean the country is doomed. How important is Mushadah, anyway? I hadn't even heard of it until the day before I went there myself. But Military Police Captain Maryanne Naro dismayingly told me the quality of the police and their station was "average." That means one of two things. Either Mushadah is more or less typical, or roughly half the Iraqi Police force is worse.

I had a much better experience when I embedded, so to speak, with the Iraqi Police in Kirkuk. I trusted the Iraqi Police in that city enough that I was willing to travel with them without any protection from the American military, even though Kirkuk is still a part of the Red Zone [unsafe areas outside the control of the multinational force]. Kirkuk, though, is an outlying case. The Iraqi Police there are Kurds. The Kurds of Iraq are the most pro-American people I have ever met in the world. They are more pro-American than Americans. There is no Kurdish insurgency, and the only Kurdish terrorist group—Ansar Al Islam, which recently changed its name to Al Qaeda in Kurdistan—is based now outside a town called Mariwan in northeastern Iran. The Iraqi Police in Kirkuk may be corrupt, but they aren't terrorists or insurgents.

The Kurds have problems of their own, even so, and not every Arab region of Iraq is the same shade of dysfunctional. Every complaint I heard about the Iraqi Army and Iraqi Police in and around Baghdad was balanced with genuine praise for the Iraqi Army and Iraqi Police in and just outside Ramadi, the capital of Anbar Province, which until recently was the most violent war-torn place in all of Iraq. If these Iraqis were typical—and make no mistake, they are not—the American military might have little reason to stay.

A Clean, Orderly Police Station

Captain Dennison and his men took me to the Al Majed station just outside the city on the banks of the Euphrates River.

"They recently changed the name," he said as we parked the Humvees outside. "The station used to have a tribal name, but they're trying to move away from that now."

The Al Majed station is so much cleaner than the one in Mushadah I could hardly believe what I was looking at.

Order and tidiness aren't everything, but police officers who live and work in a sloppy dump of a station don't inspire much confidence. If they can't clean up their own space, how can they be expected to clean up a neighborhood infested with terrorists, insurgents, and criminals? They can't, at least not in Mushadah, especially since as many as half the police themselves are terrorists, insurgents, and criminals.

The Al Majed station wasn't as clean and orderly as a hotel, but it was at least as clean and orderly as a hostel. I would have been perfectly comfortable staying there for a week. The station in Mushadah was a nasty place I couldn't wait to get out of. Even some of the American outposts in Ramadi were disgusting.

A Humvee outside the Al Majed station [sat] in a lagoon of "moon dust" that will be a lake of deep mud in the winter.

Iraqi Lieutenant Colonel Jumaa Abdul Rahman, the man in charge of Al Majed, invited me, Captain Dennison, Sergeant First Class Kitts, and First Sergeant Rodriguez into his office for tea. He sat behind his desk, and the four of us sat on couches that circled the room. A young boy brought us dark brown tea with sugar in small plastic cups.

As usual in the Middle East, the greeting ritual was considerate and elaborate. Hello. Welcome. How are you? Fine, I hope. Did you sleep well last night?

"Our success in this region is because of you," Captain Dennison said to Lieutenant Colonel Rahman. His statement was completely sincere. He was not being perfunctory or merely polite.

"And also because of you," Lieutenant Colonel Rahman said, also sincerely. "Please don't leave us."

Several minutes of idle chit chat followed, which is typical even when the real point of a meeting is business. But there didn't appear to be any business to discuss. The lieutenant colonel led us outside after awhile to admire the view of the river and the orchard of fruit trees behind the station.

Things Have Changed

"We see Iraqis smile now," Sergeant Kitts said to me on our way out. "And seeing Iraqis smile . . . that's a big deal. These people haven't had anything to smile about for a very long time. This is where we are finally earning our money."

"I agree," First Sergeant Rodriguez said. "It's a lot less volatile now, so we can actually move this place forward."

I walked among the tidy rows of grapes, figs, dates, and olives with Lieutenant Colonel Rahman and an Iraqi interpreter named Jack.

"Now that the fighting is over," I said, "what kind of work do you focus on?"

"Mainly on gathering intelligence on sleeper cells and support networks," the colonel said. "It is much easier now. People here are very appreciative and cooperative with what happened and with what is happening now. If Iraqi Police officers or coalition soldiers go to people's houses they are welcomed with open arms for food and for tea. Before the people here were not allowed to even look at coalition forces or they would be murdered by Al Qaeda."

A Pledge to Iraq's New Police Force

The United States will provide Iraq with almost $1 billion for training and technical assistance to you, the Iraqi police. We will also spend over $1.3 billion on courts, prisons, judicial protection and training and other activities related to the administration of justice and the rule of law.

You are the guardians of Iraq's future. We will stand with you after June 30 [2004] when an Iraqi government will become sovereign. Like you, we have shed our blood to construct a better, more just Iraq, an Iraq where all live in dignity.

L. Paul Bremer, speech,
Iraq Police Academy Commencement,
April 1, 2004. http://usinfo.state.gov.

"What do you think about the possibility of Americans withdrawing their forces?" I said. He had already said please don't leave us to Captain Dennison, but I wanted at least a little elaboration.

"That is not in the best interests of Iraq right now," he said. "We need some more time. If they pull out there will be a real possibility of serious sectarian warfare. Anbar is secure. Only Baghdad and the surrounding area remains to be secured. As soon as that happens, the fight will be over." He is right to suggest that most of the violence is in the Baghdad area and its surroundings. But it's still game-on in Mosul and in parts of Diyala Province. Southern Iraq suffers a lot less violence than the center, but Shia militias still control parts of it.

Gung Ho Anti-Terrorists

"Are you optimistic?" I said.

"Yes," he said.

"Why?" I said.

"I'll tell you why," he said. "I could not even dream of seeing what has taken place here in Anbar. Couldn't even dream of it. If in Anbar, why not in Baghdad?"

"Baghdad is hard," I said. "It is so much more complicated than here."

"Yes," he said and nodded. "Here we are strictly anti-terrorist. In Baghdad the police still favor their sectarian militias."

I asked Captain Dennison if American troops were still needed in Ramadi, which has not only been cleared of terrorists and insurgents but transformed into one of the most staunchly anti-terrorist communities in the world.

"We still take care of around 80 percent of the logistics for the Iraqi Army and Iraqi Police here," he said. "They're doing great work, but they still need some help getting organized."

"What are we doing here today, anyway?" I said. "Do you have anything to do here at the station?" So far all the Americans had done is say hi to the Iraqis and show me around.

"We're just checking in," he said. "The Police Transition Teams are out here training them to do slower more normal police work, less kicking in doors and beating up bad guys. The Iraqi Police are still in a bit of shock from the hell of a few months ago. They are definitely gung ho anti-terrorists. If anything, at this point, they need to dial it back."

Ramadi Is Secure

Until recently the Iraqi Police in Ramadi were more like soldiers than police officers. They weren't issuing traffic tickets or doing slow procedural work. They were fighting terrorists in a war zone that was every bit as bad as the one in Fallujah just down the road.

"It's been four months since a single mortar round hit the station," Captain Dennison said. "None of the Americans or the Iraqis out here have been in a fire fight for several months." This was in early August [2007].

There wasn't much dramatic to see or do. Counter-insurgency soldiers often go into hostile areas looking for fights that draw combatants into the open where they can be captured or killed. But the Americans and Iraqis couldn't find a fight in Ramadi now if they tried. So they do not try.

What can I say about Iraqis and Americans who cooperate with each other professionally and have their act together while ironing out minor problems? Peace is much harder to cover than war. Not much of note happens. Once again, I understood why war correspondents write off Ramadi as boring and why major networks don't broadcast from there. . . .

Dedicated and Reliable

"We went from having 200 police officers last year to having 8,000 today," Major Lee Peters said. "And that's not counting those with the orange bands." The men who wear orange bands instead of blue uniforms are semi-official community watchmen who were deputized by the tribal authorities. The people of Anbar [Province] want another layer of hyper-local security in a province Al Qaeda desperately wants to reconquer after their humiliating eviction.

I attended a brief ceremony where hundreds of newly minted Iraqi Police officers graduated.

Some finished the training and are still waiting to be formally hired. Each unit marched around the room a little bit awkwardly. They looked a bit like amateurs, but everyone who said anything about them insists they are dedicated and reliable.

"We worry about potential future infiltration by AQI," or Al Qaeda in Iraq, Colonel John Charlton said. "But we're very certain this is not a problem right now. The tribal influence on IPs [Iraqi Police] is strong. Every single one of the tribal leaders is against AQI. In Anbar Province it is very shameful and dishonorable to be a terrorist or an insurgent."

Captain Dennison also took me to the Farraj police station just outside Ramadi in an area that was sort of a suburb and sort of the countryside. . . .

"The Farraj station doesn't skim the money we give them," Lieutenant Schnitker said, "if that's what you're asking. We monitor it closely enough that we know they aren't corrupt. I can say this with confidence. We use to cut them checks, but there's no bank in Ramadi anymore. It got robbed twice, and that was it. It literally got robbed out of existence. There is no insurance in Iraq, let alone anything like FDIC. So we give them cash, and we watch how they spend it."

Iraqi Police Colonel Saidi Saleh Mohammad al Farraji, who long ago was a captain in Saddam's army, invited me and the American officers for lunch in his office. The usual Iraqi fare was served—chicken and lamb kebabs with bread, fried tomatoes, and salad.

"What's your biggest challenge," I said to the colonel, "now that Al Qaeda is gone?"

"It was counter-terrorism," he said. "Now we just need to make sure the area stays secure so they don't come back. We have sources in the community who will tell us if they come back. Civilians cooperate with us now, but they didn't before we built this station. They didn't feel safe."

"Almost all [Iraqi soldiers] said the time when the Iraqi Army can stand alone as a national defense force is still years away."

The Iraqi Army Is Not Ready to Fight

Campbell Robertson

In the viewpoint that follows, Campbell Robertson reports that the Iraqi army is willing but lacks the readiness to protect its homeland. Quoting the complaints of Iraqi officers, Robertson relates that the Iraqis lack military vehicles and up-to-date infantry weapons. On top of these shortages, Robertson cites a poor command structure that restricts the effectiveness of the fighting forces. For these reasons, many Iraqis expect that the coalition forces will remain in Iraq for some time to secure Iraq from all threats. Campbell Robertson is a New York Times *reporter covering Iraq.*

As you read, consider the following questions:

1. What types of battlefield equipment does Robertson say Iraqi units lack?

2. What is the "tough-love" approach that American military officials have taken with their Iraqi counterparts?

3. According to Robertson, what accounts for the lack of direction and coordination from higher levels in the Iraqi military command structure?

Ahmed Mahmoud, a lieutenant in the Iraqi Army, lost one leg fighting the insurgency and says he would not quit his job even if he lost the other. He believes in his army.

But asked whether that army is ready as a national defense force, capable of protecting Iraq's borders without American support, Lieutenant Mahmoud gestures toward his battalion's parking lot. A fifth of the vehicles are rotting trucks and bomb-demolished Humvees that, for some complicated bureaucratic reason, are still considered operational.

"In your opinion," Lieutenant Mahmoud says, "do you think I could fight an army with those trucks?"

The Army Needs More Time

While Americans and Iraqi civilians alike are increasingly eager to see combat operations turned over to the Iraqi Army, interviews with more than a dozen Iraqi soldiers and officers in Diyala Province, at the outset of a large-scale operation against insurgents led by Iraqis but backed by Americans, reveal a military confident of its progress but unsure of its readiness.

The army has made huge leaps forward, most of the soldiers agreed, and can hold its own in battles with the insurgency with little or no American support. But almost all said the time when the Iraqi Army can stand alone as a national defense force is still years away.

"You can't go from a lieutenant all the way to a general at once," said one Iraqi officer who spoke on condition of anonymity because he was not authorized to speak to the news media. "The army needs more time."

While the infantry is strong enough, Iraq needs viable artillery units, armored divisions, air force support and more reliable battlefield equipment, the officers said, plus the training all that requires. The soldiers and officers are for the most part zealously patriotic, but their zeal is tempered by the knowledge that they are the ones who may face the armies of neighboring countries, like Iran, after American combat forces withdraw.

Why the Coalition Forces Must Stay

"It is 2008," said Lt. Col. Muhammad Najim Khairi, a young officer in the Third Battalion of the Iraqi Army's 19th Brigade. "We are too many years behind other countries. We need the coalition forces until 2015."

They know, too, however, that a decision about troop withdrawal could probably be made not by the military but by politicians in Baghdad or Washington, representing the wishes of voters impatient with the allies' presence. Already there has been talk from Iraq's Prime Minister Nuri Kamal al-Maliki and the presumptive Democratic presidential nominee, Senator Barack Obama, of a withdrawal of American combat troops by 2010.

There are a number of ways a post-withdrawal Iraq could look, including with staffed American bases or promises of American military support in a crisis. But the current political trend from the Iraqi side is to make the imprint of foreign troops as small as possible as soon as possible, or at least to make it appear as small as possible while keeping options open for any emergency.

Tough-Love Realities

With this in mind, some American military officers in Diyala have been trying a tough-love approach. Transition teams working with Iraqi units offer advice and training but have sharply cut back logistical support.

Iraqi Army Lacks Advantages of American Counterparts

In stark contrast to American soldiers, all of whom have their own body armor, many Iraqi soldiers share a limited number of armor vests and often go without. And while U.S. forces travel in up-armored Humvees, Strykers and other armored vehicles that protect them from snipers and roadside bombs, Iraqi forces rely on trucks—or simply walk.

On March 25, 2005, near Qayyarah in northwestern Iraq, 25th Infantry Division 2nd Lt. Tom Burns led a joint American-Iraqi patrol looking for smugglers and insurgents. The Americans were in two speedy, heavily armored Stryker vehicles; the Iraqis trailed behind in battered pickup trucks. Every couple of miles, the Strykers had to idle to let the pickups catch up.

David Axe, "Experts Say Iraqi Forces Not Ready,"
June 23, 2006. www.military.com.

"It came up within the first 30 minutes of conversation" with an Iraqi officer said Capt. Bob West, an officer in a military transition team that calls itself Team McLovin. "I'm not giving you a thing, I said. The time for the U.S. forces to hold your hand is over."

For the most part, other team members said, the warning is barely acknowledged.

"I don't even know if that part gets translated," Captain West said.

But it sinks in, quietly.

The headquarters of the Fourth Battalion, to which Lieutenant Mahmoud belongs, is a complex of low white buildings that used to be a veterinary hospital. Inside one of the buildings, a group of officers gathered on a recent day to discuss issues with Maj. Jon Lauer, chief of a transition team working with the 19th Brigade, another advocate of the tough-love approach.

These discussions boil down to one complaint: that the Americans have stopped providing them with batteries, fuel, tires and other basic equipment they need, and that the Iraqi military authorities have not picked up the slack.

That led Lieutenant Mahmoud to say that because of corruption and logistical problems this army was years away from being able to protect the country on its own. The Iraqi Army, he said, is up to the task but lacking the tools.

Leadership Problems

Americans who work closely with Iraqi units have a slightly different diagnosis. The need for state-of-the-art military equipment is overstated, they say. Costly and complicated maintenance often make it more trouble than it is worth. And, they say, rumors of rampant corruption along the supply lines usually turn out to be worse than reality.

They point out that good equipment often ends up sitting unused in plain sight, like the brand new, air-conditioned, reinforced bunkers huddled in a corner of a parking lot at the 19th Brigade headquarters.

Rather, they say, a major problem is lack of direction and coordination from higher levels.

That is to be expected in a young army being built from the ground up, particularly because the higher ranks are filled with veterans of Saddam Hussein's rigid command structure.

"When you grow up in a very regimented system the lower you go, the easier it is to train," said Lt. Col. Tony Aguto, an officer with the Second Stryker Cavalry Regiment, the main American force in the Diyala operation. "As you go up, it gets more difficult."

An Army Unsure of Its Mission

The Third and Fourth battalions, which cover the southwestern corner of Diyala as part of the 19th Brigade, are two of the best in the province, American officers in the region say. But they often have to act without guidance. Areas of Diyala heavy with insurgent traffic sit unpatrolled because the battalions are not told who is in charge of what.

"I've asked them what their mission is, and they don't know," Major Lauer said.

If there is anyone who understands these problems, it is Col. Ali Mahmoud, commander of the 19th Brigade's Third Battalion.

The Americans in the region consider the wry, soft-spoken Colonel Mahmoud, 41, one of the most valuable officers in Diyala. Conferring all night on his cell phone with tribal sheiks, Colonel Mahmoud believes that a battle is won as much by force as by a good relationship with the local people. A Sunni who has surrounded himself with Shiite and Kurdish officers, he believes that an effective Iraqi Army is one with a thorough sectarian mix.

Because of his successful approach, he runs one of the few battalions in Diyala that does not have its own dedicated American military transition team.

But Colonel Mahmoud is more pessimistic than most about an Iraqi future without American combat troops.

"Believe me," he said. "There will be a big disaster."

No Choice but to Fight

Sitting at his headquarters, Colonel Mahmoud sees signs of the future: continuing supply problems and the involvement of Iran in Iraqi affairs. When his troops come across insurgents' weapons caches, they sometimes find what he says are Iranian weapons that are more up to date than anything in his arsenal.

"The Iranian side will play their game," he said with a tone of resignation, "once the coalition forces pull out."

But just a few hours later Colonel Mahmoud was on the road in the early light of day, leading a five-hour patrol south of Baquba, once swarming with insurgents. Asked why he keeps working against the militias every day, given how futile he thinks it might all be, he said he had no choice.

"I don't want those guys to continue working to give Iraq away," he said.

| "New equipment is pouring into the Iraqi army, including weapons, radios and transportation."

The Iraqi Army Will Soon Be Ready to Fight

C. Todd Lopez

In the following viewpoint, C. Todd Lopez explains how the Iraqi army is rebuilding its strength while fighting the insurgency in Iraq. According to Lopez, the Iraqis are getting new equipment that is helping them defeat the enemy, and their recent successes have bought them time to engage in much-needed collective unit training. Although Lopez reports that the Iraqi army still faces shortcomings, he acknowledges that the units have progressed well in a short time. Staff Sergeant C. Todd Lopez is a writer for the U.S. Air Force American Forces Press Service.

As you read, consider the following questions:

1. As Lopez states, by what percent has the Iraqi army grown between 2007 and 2008?
2. What is the Warfighter Program, as Lopez describes it?

C. Todd Lopez, "Iraqi Army Shows Great Growth in Year," army.mil, June 26, 2008. Reproduced by permission.

3. In what two key areas does Brigadier General Steven
   Salazar think the Iraqi army still must improve?

The Iraqi army has grown by 60 percent in the last year
[2007–2008], and stands now at nearly 180,000 soldiers.
The army is also now training its own soldiers, and its effectiveness in combat has allowed it to concentrate more on improving logistics and supply chains.

Brig. Gen. Steven L. Salazar said that during the last year,
the Iraqi army has built up internal momentum and has taken
the reins for themselves on many soldier training functions.

"More and more the Iraqis are doing training for themselves now," Salazar said.

He serves as deputy commanding general, Coalition Army
Advisory Training Team, Multi-National Security Transition
Command-Iraq. The organization is responsible for training
and equipping the Iraqi army.

Time for Training at All Levels

"Basic training is conducted by the Iraqi army, military occu-
pational specialty qualification training is conducted by the
Iraqi army, and noncommissioned officer [NCO] training—at
all three levels—is being conducted by the Iraqi army now," he
added.

The NCO training conducted now in Iraq includes a
corporal's course, a sergeant's course, and a squad leader's
course. New to the regiment is a master instructor course also
taught by Iraqi army NCOs. Similarly, officer courses are also
being conducted by the Iraqi army.

New equipment is pouring into the Iraqi army, including
weapons, radios and transportation. At the Iraqi Army Service
Support Institute, level-3 maintenance and support soldiers
are now being trained to repair that new equipment.

"Those soldiers will tell you they can take an entire Humvee apart down to nothing and put it back together," he said.

"They can take generators apart and put them back together as well. And at the bomb disposal school they are taking damaged robots—part of the bomb disposal companies in the Iraqi army—and completely repairing them and putting them back into the fight."

Soon, said Salazar, the new army will also engage in collective unit training. The Warfighter Program will take battalions of Iraqi army soldiers out of the fight and into centers where they can conduct "home station training" in much the same way U.S. soldiers do.

"This is really a milestone I think, and the beginning of something big as we transition from the counter-insurgency fight to ultimately an army that is conducting training," Salazar said.

Taking time to train is a kind of luxury for Iraqi soldiers, who have been embroiled in the fight. But it is their efforts, said Salazar, that enabled them to create that opportunity.

"We have been so busy with fighting the insurgency that there really has been little or no time for conducting training at a larger organizational level," he said. "But thanks to the success of the Iraqi operations, which has created such a low-level of violence, we are now ready for (the Warfighter Program.)"

New Equipment, Better Morale

During upcoming unit training, Iraqi soldiers may have the opportunity to use some of the new equipment the army has procured, including 80,000 new M-16 rifles; 8,500 refurbished Humvee vehicles; and more than 12,000 Single-Channel Ground-Air Radio Systems, or SINGARS radios. The systems have been procured either through the Iraqi Security Forces Fund, or through foreign military sales.

But the new equipment has great impact on the way the Iraqi army operates and is perceived by the public. It also has a great effect on soldier morale, Salazar said.

Assessment of the Independent Commission on the Security Forces in Iraq

In general, the Iraqi Army and Special Forces are becoming more proficient in counterinsurgency and counterterrorism operations; they are gaining size and strength, and will increasingly be capable of assuming greater responsibility for Iraq's security. The Special Forces brigade is highly capable and extremely effective. It is trained in counterterrorism and it is assessed to be the best element of the new Iraqi military.

The Iraqi Army possesses an adequate supply of willing and able manpower, a steadily improving basic training capability, and equipment tailored to counterinsurgency operations. There is evidence to show that the emerging Iraqi soldier is willing to fight against the declared enemies of the state, with some exceptions remaining along ethnic lines. The Army is making efforts to reduce sectarian influence within its ranks and achieving some progress. The Army's operational effectiveness is increasing; yet it will continue to rely on help in areas such as command and control, equipment, fire support, logistical support, intelligence, and transportation. Despite continued progress, the Iraqi military will not be ready to independently fulfill its security role within the next 12 to 18 months. Nevertheless, the Commission believes that substantial progress can be achieved within that period of time.

James L. Jones, The Report of the Independent Commission of the Security Forces of Iraq, *September 6, 2007.*

"When you see a group of Iraqi soldiers driving around in a Humvee, and they get to operate it with their own markings on it, the Iraqi flag on it, it does a tremendous amount for the pride of the Iraqi soldier and consequently his performance," Salazar said. "It also has a tremendous impact on the local population as they see their soldiers operating this kind of professional modern equipment. So what these purchases do for the Iraqi army are really tremendous."

Room for Improvement

Salazar said the Iraqi army has shown more independence in conducting large operations in places like Basra, Sadr City, Mosul and Al Amara. But the service still must work on two key areas. The first, he said is enabler elements.

"We built a tremendous maneuver capability with considerable combat power in the Iraqi army based on the number of battalions and brigades—up to 13 divisions," he said. "We still need to grow those enablers, such as intelligence, surveillance and reconnaissance formations and engineer formations."

Salazar also said the Iraqi army must work on stronger logistics. To aid in that effort, the coalition is working to provide logistics facilities for each Iraqi army division. They are also in the process of building national depots, including the Taji National Depot to provide national-level maintenance, and the Taji National Supply Depot.

"Those are in the process of being built and will be complete by and large by the end of this year," he said. "We expect self sustainment, in terms of logistics by the middle of 2009."

Despite growing pains, Salazar said the Iraqi army is impressive and that those soldiers are driven by many of the same things as American soldiers.

"I think the Iraqi army has been tremendously successful," he said. "You can see evidence of that by the successful operations taking place—there is still a considerable threat out there. And in many aspects those soldiers are much like the American soldiers. They have a sense of duty and country, also a sense of economics and an aspiration for opportunity. I think what most Iraqis see is opportunity to serve their nation and to support their families."

Periodical Bibliography

The following articles have been selected to supplement the diverse views presented in this chapter.

Nouri al-Maliki
"Our Strategy for a Democratic Iraq," *Washington Post*, June 9, 2006.

Paul L. Bremer III
"Baghdad Must Pay Its Way," *New York Times*, May 4, 2008.

Antonio Castaneda
"Are Iraqi Police Ready to Take Over?" *Deseret News*, December 11, 2005.

Charles Crain
"Iraq's New Job Insecurity," *Time*, December 24, 2007.

Francis Fukuyama
"Iraq May Be Stable, But the War Was a Mistake," *Wall Street Journal*, August 15, 2008.

Peter Grier
"How Will the Iraq War End?" *Christian Science Monitor*, March 18, 2008.

Abigail Hauslohner
"Has al-Maliki Turned on the U.S.?" *Time*, July 8, 2008.

Frederick W. Kagan
"Reconcilable Differences," *Weekly Standard*, November 2007.

Rod Nordland and Christopher Dickey
"Tribe Versus Tribe," *Newsweek*, January 24, 2005.

Richard A. Oppel Jr., Sabrina Tavernise, and Qais Mizher
"Military Officials Add to U.S. Criticism of Iraq's Government," *New York Times*, September 28, 2006.

Campbell Robertson and Riyadh Mohammed
"Violent Iraqi Government Raid Threatens to Inflame Province's Sectarian Tensions," *New York Times*, August 20, 2008.

Megan Scully
"GAO: Iraq Government Failing Most Congressional Goals," *Congress Daily*, September 4, 2007.

**OPPOSING VIEWPOINTS® SERIES**

CHAPTER 2

Should Iraq Be Partitioned into Ethnic States?

Chapter Preface

Former U.S. diplomat and advocate of an independent Kurdish nation in the Middle East, Peter Galbraith stated in a May 2007 article that "Iraq is not salvageable as a unitary state." Like many who favor the partition of Iraq into ethnic and sectarian states, Galbraith views Iraq as a Muslim collective already divided among the Shiite Arabs in the south, Sunni Arabs in the middle, and the Kurds in the north. Former Iraqi regimes—including the recently deposed rule of Saddam Hussein—these observers say, have forced the three peoples of Iraq into one nation largely through oppressive statecraft. And without a repressive central government, it is likely that the three Iraqs cannot live easily as one.

Some see a "hard" partition of Iraq as inevitable. That is, they assume the three distinct states cannot work together and must be arbitrarily divided into autonomous nations—in the same manner that the former Yugoslavia was divided after civil war. In fact, hard partition pessimists suggest that civil war in Iraq is already in progress and can only be ended when the newly realized Sunni, Shiite, and Kurdish states fix borders.

On the other hand, many of those who believe a full-scale civil war can be avoided are pressing for the United States to oversee the "soft" partition of Iraq. Galbraith, for one, supports a loose federalist structure for Iraq that puts minimal power in a central government and creates three semi-autonomous regions around the ethnic and sectarian divisions. The point of soft partition is to keep some semblance of a unified Iraq intact because, as conservative *Washington Post* columnist Charles Krauthammer maintains, "de jure partition into separate states would invite military intervention by the neighbors—Turkey, Iran, Saudi Arabia and Syria."

Opponents of any form of partition also argue different points of view. Stephen Schwart, a contributor to the *Weekly Standard*, asserts that access to water and oil—the basis of Iraq's economy—are not evenly divided among the proposed states, inviting further feuding and economic instability. Furthermore, he claims that "mixed families and villages would be even more violently divided by partition, exacting psychological injuries for generations to come." Schwartz insists that the future of Iraq belongs with the Iraqis and that partition can only come from within and not be imposed or managed by foreigners.

Others in the non-partition camp do not want to waste the progress made in restoring a central government. Army Lieutenant Colonel James A. Gavrilis, a Special Forces officer who works on Iraq issues for the Joint Chiefs of Staff, believes the democratic revolution in Iraq has not yet run its course. He states, "The potential for civil war is there, certainly, but it is not as far as many are claiming. We have not seen indicators of full-scale civil war or mass mobilizations or a collapse of politics." Even Iraqi leaders from Sunni and Shiite political parties have stated their opposition to partition, arguing that division would likely inflame tensions, not end them. They insist that Iraq must work through its own problems before it can emerge a stronger, unified state.

The authors of the viewpoints in the following chapter elucidate some of the aforementioned arguments and exemplify the debate that still surrounds the notion of a partitioned Iraq.

| *"A soft partition model may be the only hope for avoiding an all-out civil war."*

Iraq Should Be Partitioned

Edward P. Joseph and Michael E. O'Hanlon

In the following viewpoint, Edward P. Joseph and Michael E. O'Hanlon contend that because current attempts to restore authority to a centralized government in Baghdad are failing to quell intersectarian violence, the best hope to bring peace to Iraq is to partition the country along ethnic and sectarian lines. Joseph and O'Hanlon acknowledge that partitioning Iraq into Shiite, Sunni, and Kurdish states may not be popular or easy, but with sectarian regions beginning to solidify and ethnic cleansing on the rise, the only viable solution that would avoid civil war is to carve Iraq up and then work on measures to secure boundaries, share oil revenues among the regions, and bring about regional stability. Edward P. Joseph is a scholar and visiting lecturer at the Paul H. Nitze School of Advanced International Studies at Johns Hopkins University in Washington, D.C. Michael O'Hanlon is a senior fellow at the Brookings Institution, an independent public policy research organization.

Note to readers: This paper was conceived in 2006 and written in late 2006/early 2007. At that time, Iraq was in the throes of civil war. The United States and the Iraqi government were perilously close to military defeat, and the project of building a new, stable, multiethnic, and cohesive Iraq was dangerously close to complete failure. Some Iraqi voices recognized as much and also favored consideration of enhanced federalism; they included many Kurds and the so-called ISCI party. Most Iraqis still opposed the idea, and it would only have been viable if they had changed their views, to be sure. But dismissing the option of such enhanced federalism out of hand would have been a mistake given the lack of good alternatives. Our paper was designed to help flesh out the implications and mechanics of enhanced federalism/soft partition in case that was useful to any Iraqis and others who might have wanted to consider the option. I no longer support soft partition myself; the remarkable success of the population-protection strategy of General Petraeus over the last two years, combined with impressive political progress by the Iraqi government, makes it unnecessary at this point. It would never have been a panacea, never have been easy to implement, and would only have been feasible with fairly robust and widespread Iraqi support. But to dismiss the notion of considering such an option back when Iraq was in a lethal civil war killing at least 50,000 a year and driving 100,000 a month from their homes would have been to deprive policy makers of an important option when the strategy of the day was demonstrably failing. I am delighted to see that, against the odds, the surge strategy worked so well. And I would concede that it was preferable to soft partition; in fact, I supported the surge once it was proposed in late 2006, even as I envisioned the possibility that it would fail. The soft partition proposal was offered as a contingency plan in case it was needed, not as a preferred choice. Helping policymakers flesh out and assess such options is an important role of scholars and I stand by the fact that Mr. Joseph and I did so, even as I no longer believe this type of option will be needed in Iraq.

As you read, consider the following questions:

1. Why do Joseph and O'Hanlon believe that Kurds and Shi'i Arabs might be willing to share oil revenues under a partition plan?

2. How many Iraqis are already being displaced from their homes every month, according to the authors?

3. Why do Joseph and O'Hanlon suggest that foreign troop levels in Iraq may not immediately decrease if partition plans are put in place?

The time may be approaching when the only hope for a more stable Iraq is a soft partition of the country. Soft partition would involve the Iraqis, with the assistance of the international community, dividing their country into three main regions. Each would assume primary responsibility for its own security and governance, as Iraqi Kurdistan already does. Creating such a structure could prove difficult and risky. However, when measured against the alternatives—continuing to police an ethno-sectarian war, or withdrawing and allowing the conflict to escalate—the risks of soft partition appear more acceptable. Indeed, soft partition in many ways simply responds to current realities on the ground, particularly since the February 2006 bombing of the Samarra mosque, a major Shi'i shrine, dramatically escalated intersectarian violence. If the U.S. troop surge, and the related effort to broker political accommodation through the existing coalition government of Prime Minister Nuri al-Maliki fail, soft partition may be the only means of avoiding an intensification of the civil war and growing threat of a regional conflagration [conflict]. While most would regret the loss of a multi-ethnic, diverse Iraq, the country has become so violent and so divided along ethno-sectarian lines that such a goal may no longer be achievable.

Partition Is Plan B

Soft partition would represent a substantial departure from the current approach of the [George W.] Bush administration and that proposed by the Iraq Study Group, both of which envision a unitary Iraq ruled largely from Baghdad. It would require new negotiations, the formation of a revised legal framework for the country, the creation of new institutions at the regional level, and the organized but voluntary movement of populations. For these reasons, we refer to it as a "Plan B" for Iraq. It would require acquiescence from most major Iraqi political factors (though not necessarily all, which is an unrealistic standard in any event). It might best be negotiated outside the current Iraqi political process, perhaps under the auspices of a special representative of the United Nations as suggested by Carlos Pascual of the Brookings Institution.

Mediating an End to Conflict

International mediation could succeed where the current, U.S.-led effort to pry concessions out of al-Maliki's government has failed. Indeed, Kurds and Shi'i Arabs would have far more incentive to cede on the fundamental issue of oil production and revenue-sharing if they knew that their core strategic objectives would be realized through secure, empowered regions. Although it would surely play a facilitating role along with the United Nations, the United States need not bear the burden, nor the stigma, of leading Iraqis towards soft partition. At the outset, it would suffice for the United States simply to cease its insistence on the alternative of an Iraq ruled from Baghdad that at once fails to serve Sunni Arabs while serving as a symbolic threat to Shi'i Arabs—an Iraq that has encouraged the Shi'i Arabs to cement their dominance of the country's power center against any potential Sunni Arab revival.

Soft partition has a number of advantages over other "Plan B" proposals currently under discussion. Most others focus on a U.S. troop withdrawal or on the containment of civil war spillover to other countries, rather than the prevention of a substantial worsening of Iraq's civil war. Soft partition could allow the United States and its partners to preserve their core

Decentralization Is Already Underway

Decentralization [in Iraq] is hardly as radical as it may seem: The Iraqi Constitution, in fact, already provides for a federal structure and a procedure for provinces to combine into regional governments. . . .

Some will say moving toward strong regionalism would ignite sectarian cleansing. But that's exactly what is going on already, in ever-bigger waves. Others will argue that it would lead to partition. But a breakup is already under way. As it was in Bosnia, a strong federal system is a viable means to prevent both perils in Iraq.

Joseph R. Biden Jr. and Leslie H. Gelb,
New York Times, *May 1, 2006.*

strategic goals: An Iraq that lives in peace with its neighbors, opposes terrorism, and gradually progresses towards a more stable future. It would further allow for the possibility over time for the reestablishment of an Iraq increasingly integrated across sectarian lines rather than permanently segregated. If carefully implemented, it would help end the war and the enormous loss of life on all sides.

Managing Ethnic Relaxation

Such a plan for soft partition (as opposed to hard-partition which involves the outright division of Iraq) is consistent with the plan of Senator Joseph Biden (D-Delaware) and Leslie Gelb, a former President of the Council on Foreign Relations. Our plan builds upon their proposal, setting out the full rationale for such an approach as well as the means by which this new regionalized political system would be implemented through soft partition. Those means include creating processes to help people voluntarily relocate to parts of Iraq where they would no longer be in the minority, and hence where they should be safer. This is not an appealing prospect to put it mildly. However, if the choice becomes sustaining a failing U.S. troop surge or abandoning Iraq altogether, with all the risks that entails in terms of intensified violence and regional turmoil, then soft partition might soon become the least bad option. The question will then be less whether it is morally and strategically acceptable, and more whether it is achievable. . . .

Sunni and Shi'i Arabs have traditionally opposed partition, whether hard or soft. However, with 50,000 to 100,000 persons being displaced from their homes and several thousand losing their lives every month, sectarian identities are hardening as ethno-sectarian separation is increasing. In short, Iraq today increasingly resembles Bosnia-Herzegovina (hereafter Bosnia) in the early 1990s, where one of us worked extensively. While Iraq may not yet resemble Bosnia in 1995 in which ethnic separation had progressed to the point where fairly clear regional borders could be established, it is well beyond the Bosnia of 1992 when the separation was just beginning. Moreover, while Bosnia eventually wound up as a reasonably stable federation, as many as 200,000 may have lost their lives before that settlement. A comparable per capita casualty toll in Iraq would imply one million dead. It should be the goal of policy makers to avoid such a calamity by trying to manage the ethnic relocation process, if it becomes unstoppable, rather than allow terrorists and militias to use violence to drive this process to its grim, logical conclusion.

What Partition Entails

To make soft partition viable, several imposing practical challenges must be addressed. These include sharing oil revenue among the regions, creating reasonably secure boundaries between them, and restructuring the international troop presence. Helping minority populations relocate if they wish requires a plan for providing security to those who are moving as well as those left behind. That means the international troop presence will not decline immediately, although we estimate that it could be reduced substantially within eighteen months or so. Population movements also necessitate housing swaps and job creation programs.

Soft partition cannot be imposed from the outside. Indeed, it need not be. Iraq's new constitution, approved by plebiscite in October 2005, already permits the creation of "regions." Still, a framework for soft partition would go much further than Iraq has to date. Among other things, it would involve the organized movement of two million to five million Iraqis, which could only happen safely if influential leaders encouraged their supporters to cooperate, and if there were a modicum of agreement on where to draw borders and how to share oil revenue.

The Right Time for Partition

As noted, unless the U.S. troop surge succeeds dramatically, a soft partition model may be the only hope for avoiding an all-out civil war. Indeed, even if the surge achieves some positive results, the resulting political window might best be used to negotiate and implement soft partition. As of writing, it is too soon to know exactly how the current approach will fare. We are highly skeptical of its prospects. But one need not have a final assessment of the surge to begin considering which "Plan B" might succeed it in the event of failure—or even of a partial but insufficient success.

> *"Partitionist quick-fixes designed along unimaginative ethno-religious lines would pull in the opposite direction of coexistence. They would constitute a cowardly cave-in to those foreign terrorists who for three years straight have unsuccessfully tried to blow up the sturdy social fabric of Iraq."*

Iraq Should Not Be Partitioned

Reidar Visser

In the following viewpoint, Reidar Visser argues that attempts to partition Iraq are doomed to failure because, contrary to Western foreign policy beliefs, Iraq has a strong nationalist identity. According to Visser, allegiances in Iraq are not sectarian or ethnic, so plans to fracture Iraq into sectarian districts will run into stiff resistance. Visser suggests that Western powers leave the Iraqis to work out their own coexistence as they have done for centuries. Reidar Visser is a research fellow at the Norwegian Institute of International Affairs. He is also the author of Basra, the Failed Gulf State: Separatism and Nationalism in Southern Iraq.

Reidar Visser, "Iraq's Partition Fantasy," *openDemocracy*, May 18, 2006. Reproduced by permission.

As you read, consider the following questions:

1. As Visser explains, what faction in Iraq has been promoting federalism in Iraq and why?

2. How do most Iraqis identify themselves to Western journalists, according to Visser, and why does Visser see this as significant?

3. What problems does Visser believe are inherent in the Iraqi constitution's allowance for federalism?

A feature of political discussion of Iraq in recent weeks [Spring 2006] has been another flurry of propaganda by United States politicians in favour of dividing Iraq into three statelets or semi-independent federal entities. "Soft partition", "controlled division" or an "extension of the federal idea to the Sunni community" are but a few of the euphemisms that have been marshalled in support of this sort of exercise.

The schemes are strikingly similar, and their proponents indefatigable: Iraq is dismissed as an "artificial entity"; its "proper" and "natural" constituent components are instead identified as three ethno-religious communities—Shi'a Arabs, Sunni Arabs and Kurds.

In fact, Iraqi history fails to support such ideas—and particularly the notion that it should be necessary to enforce barriers between the Sunni and Shi'a Arabs. Quite the contrary, if the pundits who urge partition had bothered to check what actually happened when centrifugal forces were pushed to the maximum in the south of Iraq in the 1920s, they would have seen that regionalism, not sectarianism, has historically been the main competitor to Iraqi nationalism south of Baghdad— and a feeble one at that.

The idea of tripartite break-up, on the other hand finds little resonance in Iraqi history. In testimony to their sublime artificiality, contemporary partitionist misnomers like "Shi'istan" and "Sunnistan" are altogether absent from the historical record; like much of the pro-partition advocacy they exist solely in the minds of outsiders who base their entire argument on far-fetched parallels to European political experiences.

Basra's Precedent

In the early 1920s, for the first and so far the only time in Iraqi history, an actual attempt at separating the south from Baghdad was launched. This came soon after Britain had initiated a mandate administration to prepare the former Ottoman provinces of Basra, Baghdad and Mosul for nationhood as a unitary state. But the composition of the southern separatist elite of the 1920s—and the geographical scope of their project—should give today's partitionists pause for thought.

For this was not a clergy-driven attempt at establishing some sort of Shi'a state. Instead, it was a scheme to create a small merchant republic on the banks of the Shatt al-Arab, a pro-British enclave that would cover Basra and the strategic coastal strip between the Gulf and the delta of the great Mesopotamian rivers north to Qurna only.

Moreover, it was an emphatically cosmopolitan enterprise: Arabs, Persians, Indians and Jews came together in pursuit of the Basra separatist movement. Sunni Arab emigrants from Najd were the moving spirits. The Shi'a Arabs, for their part, actually had their greatest numerical strength in the vast former Ottoman province of Baghdad (and not in Basra, as many of today's partitionists seem to believe); apart from a few pro-separation figures based in the immediate vicinity of the city of Basra they remained totally aloof from the secessionist bid.

A Movement Without Popular Support

Even though it constituted the most concerted domestic "southern" challenge to the territorial integrity of Iraq in 20th-century history, the Basra separation movement ended in fiasco. The separatists were the richest men of Basra—owners of enormous tracts of fertile date gardens and successful businessmen with networks extending into other parts of the world—and yet, they were unable to muster popular support for their daring enterprise.

Who was their enemy? An authoritarian regime in Baghdad with the military means to drive home its own megalomaniac ideas about Iraqi nationalism? A British colonial machine with a singularity of purpose so entrenched as to make impossible any challenges to London's preferred vision of a unified Iraq? Far from it. The Iraqi government apparatus of the 1920s was decidedly flimsy, and throughout the period of the mandate, the British would periodically contemplate scuttling "back to Basra". Both these forces would have had trouble in stemming the separatist project if it had in fact enjoyed universal local support.

No, it was the young men of Basra—impecunious and landless as they may have been—who defeated the separatist project, by presenting a competing and very different vision for the future. Many of them had been employed as civil servants in late Ottoman times, and had colleagues from the areas further north. Among themselves—and Ottoman documents prove this beyond doubt—they had referred to the territory between Basra and Samarra (and sometimes even Mosul) as "Iraq" long before 1914, quite contrary to the baseless but now widespread idea that there had been no sense of connection between Basra and Baghdad before the British.

Armed with this "Iraq" concept, the young intelligentsia converted the south to Iraqi nationalism at an early stage, with schools, newspapers and voluntary associations—not extortion or the use of force—as their principal instruments. The process was more universal in the south than in the north of Iraq, but even in the Kurdish areas there have been considerable regional variations with regard to relations with Baghdad, and in historical perspective only Sulaimaniya has an unbroken record of antipathy to the Iraqi capital.

Divisions in Iraq Are Not Sectarian

This dualism—tentative regionalisms and quite robust Iraqi nationalism—is reflected in today's situation. Once more, if enthusiastic armchair partitionists in the west had cared to investigate the specific policy proposals of their would-be "Shi'a autonomists", they would have discovered yet another misfit between their own map and the landscapes of Iraqi reality. For, contrary to what westerners commonly think, the most longstanding post-war southern challenge to the paradigm of a unitary Iraqi state structure has been of a regionalist rather than a sectarian character.

Ever since summer 2004, local politicians in the oil-rich triangle of Basra, Amara and Nasiriya have advocated the establishment of a small-scale federal entity limited to these three southernmost provinces of Iraq—in other words, a subdivision of the Shi'a territories, by Shi'a who say they have had enough of domination by other, "northern" Shi'a. The idea of a single Shi'a canton from Baghdad to the Gulf, on the other hand, is a more recent phenomenon, dating back only to summer 2005, when a caucus of Shi'a politicians from central Iraq, mostly returned exiles, began promoting it.

While western observers soon became enthralled by the project, ordinary Iraqi Shi'a have proven more difficult to convince, and grassroots activity in support of this sectarian scheme has remained limited. In the Kurdish-dominated north the urge towards autonomy is far more widespread, but here too, perceptible regional differences—in this case between east and west—remain. They pose another challenge to neat ethnic categorizations whose principal virtue seems to be their soothing effects on the minds of western politicians.

Moreover, just as in the 1920s the alternative to decentralisation—Iraqi nationalism—remains flourishing. Even today, in a climate of growing sectarian terrorism calculated to obliterate the idea of coexistence, many Iraqis stubbornly refuse to reveal their ethno-religious identity when interrogated by

An Excuse for American Domination

If Iraq were to be broken into three, the nation would be rendered toothless for all time in the same way the former Yugoslavia is today.

The US [United States] would then have an excuse to stay around in some force "to protect" such tiny fledgling states from each other and from their neighbours. In fact, it would consolidate complete domination of their oil because such small entities would no longer have a voice.

Linda S. Heard, "Let's Try Partitioning the US,"
Gulf News, *October 2, 2007.*

western journalists. Many simply say they are "Iraqis"—an answer that tends to cause consternation among interviewers who expect more specific answers.

Among several key Iraqi leaders who never went into exile abroad, the situation is much the same. "Federalism" appears not to exist in the vocabulary of the Grand Ayatollah Ali al-Sistani—who consistently emphasises national "unity" in his official pronouncements—and [Shiite leader] Muqtada al-Sadr's radical Islamism comes with a strong Iraqi nationalist component that foreigners often overlook.

Neo-Imperialism at Work in Iraq

In sum, then, the process of regionalisation in Iraq is far more tentative and open-ended than the orderly caricature maps currently bandied about in western think-tanks would indicate. But those partition schemes are more than a distortion of Iraqi history and today's realities. They also demonstrate flagrant contempt for the fragile democratic process which is underway in Iraq. This is rather ironic, given that many of those who advocate partition take pride in describing themselves as staunch opponents of "neo-imperialisms" of all descriptions.

But where many British colonial administrators at least had the tact to confine their worst excesses of impromptu line-drawing to sparsely populated desert areas, today's hobby-artists do not shy away from using even complex urban landscapes as canvas for their reckless activities. They simply do not seem to grasp the fundamentally anti-democratic nature of their demand that the Iraqis be divided into three mutually exclusive identity-categories.

An Untidy Constitutional Mechanism for Partition

A better option for westerners interested in a debate which first and foremost is an Iraqi matter would be to take note of the constitutional mechanisms already in place for delimitating future federal units—and to engage in a more gradualist fashion with the problems likely to emerge precisely because of Iraq's untidy history and lack of clear-cut ethnic fault-lines.

Article 115 of the Iraqi constitution sets out that aspirant regional entities may achieve federal status through referenda in the areas "that wish to create a region". But what if several competing visions materialise—as the complex past history would indeed seem to suggest as a likely outcome? What if Basra with its oil refineries wants to go it alone, while some in neighbouring Dhi Qar incline towards federation with their big brother, and oil-deficient Najaf would prefer to control both by using Shi'ism as political ideology?

What are the implications of the lax requirements for calling a referendum, whereby comparatively small factions in local councils or the governorate populations at large (33% and

10% respectively) may challenge existing administrative borders and launch referendums and, conceivably, counter-referenda?

And what happens if a referendum fails and Iraqi nationalism once more prevails—can the challenge to the unitary state be repeated, and if so when?

If no checks are established here, Iraqi politics might easily degenerate into a perpetual cycle of referenda, with politicians frenetically probing for facile answers in a cultural tapestry that above all has proven complex and resistant to disentanglement procedures.

Destroying Coexistence

On these and other issues, the Iraqi constitutional framework has yet to provide clear answers. This is also where outsiders interested in the Iraqi transition process should properly expend their energies and contribute to debate, instead of undemocratically enforcing their own black-and-white thinking and fully-fledged federal models on a land whose people can draw on a centuries-long local tradition of multiethnic coexistence.

Partitionist quick-fixes designed along unimaginative ethno-religious lines would pull in the opposite direction of coexistence. They would constitute a cowardly cave-in to those foreign terrorists who for three years straight have unsuccessfully tried to blow up the sturdy social fabric of Iraq. The crude maps that accompany the break-up propaganda are an affront to the complex historical experiences they claim to represent, and encapsulate a continuous and highly disturbing trend towards the complete expropriation of the Iraqi transition process.

| "A break-up of Iraq might not stop at Iraq's borders."

Partitioning Iraq Would Create Regional Instability

Juan Cole

In the viewpoint that follows, Juan Cole argues that attempts to partition Iraq into Shiite, Sunni, and Kurdish regions could lead to sectarian violence that may draw in neighboring states. In Cole's view, countries such as Iran and Syria may gain influence over the Shiite and Sunni regions, destabilizing power in the area and inviting cross-border conflicts. Juan Cole is a professor of modern Middle Eastern and South Asian history at the University of Michigan. He is also the president of the Global Americana Institute, a scholarly organization that translates major works of American democracy into various Middle Eastern languages.

As you read, consider the following questions:

1. As Cole explains, the Bush administration has likely opposed plans to partition Iraq in order to allay the fears of what two major regional U.S. allies?

Juan Cole, "Partitioning Iraq," Salon.com, October 30, 2006. This article first appeared in Salon.com, at http://www.salon.com. An online version remains in the Salon archives. Reprinted with permission.

2. What name have some pundits given to the Shiite super-province that cleric Abdul Aziz al-Hakim promotes?

3. What two regional neighbors does Cole suggest could pick up the Sunni factions that separate from a united Iraq?

The possibility that ethnic rivalries may break Iraq into three pieces has emerged as an election issue in U.S. politics. [In October 2006, George W.], Bush administration spokesman Tony Snow branded any plan for partition a "non-starter." Other politicians, however, are not so sure. Both Republicans and Democrats have endorsed a loose Iraqi federation of three equal parts, and some are even campaigning on the idea. Democratic Senate candidate Harold Ford of Tennessee and Democratic House candidate Ted Ankrum of Texas are among those who have touted versions of partition on the stump. What are the pros and cons here, and what explains George Bush's die-hard opposition?

Regional Fears of Iraq's Partition

The most determined opponents of the creation of regional confederacies in Iraq are Turkey and Saudi Arabia. The Turks fear that if there is an independent Kurdistan in Iraq's north, it will become a magnet for Turkey's own substantial and fractious minority of Kurds. Saudi Arabia, which adheres to the ultra-strict Wahhabi Sunni school of Islam, has poor relations with Shiite Iran, and traditionally had severe tensions even with its own Shiites, who form perhaps 10 percent of the Saudi population. It objects to a Shiite super-province right next door in Iraq's south.

It is likely in order not to ruffle Turkish and Saudi feathers that the Bush administration so firmly opposes all partition plans. Turkey, a NATO [North Atlantic Treaty Organization] ally of Washington, has been even more vocal and critical than Saudi Arabia about the Iraq imbroglio. But Bush and [Vice President Dick] Cheney are especially attentive to Saudi concerns. Like Riyadh, they would view an autonomous Shiite super-province, which could easily fall under the gravitational pull of Iran, as highly undesirable.

Congressional Advocates of Partition

Within Congress, however, the temptation to indulge Iraq's warring factions in their desire to divide the country has grown. The most prominent proponent of carving Iraq into three major ethnically based provinces, with regions for the Kurds, Sunni Arabs and Shiites under a weak federal umbrella, is Democratic Sen. Joseph Biden of Delaware. The idea has now been adopted by Sen. Kay Bailey Hutchison, R-Texas. She told the Texas press [in October 2006], "Yes, it would be hard to do, but it would be worth trying . . . People say, 'Well, that would balkanize the country.' Well, things are pretty stable in the Balkans right now. It's looking better than Iraq."

The senators believe that as the conflict in Iraq continues and sectarian violence mounts, trying to make Iraq's battling ethnic groups cooperate with one another in multiethnic provinces has begun to look like a mistake. But surely it is the souring of the U.S. electorate on the war and the need of election campaigns to sketch out distinctive positions and realistic solutions to the crisis that in some part impels U.S. politicians to turn to this desperate expedient.

Within Iraq, Biden and Hutchison are echoed by the Kurds and by Shiite cleric Abdul Aziz al-Hakim, the leader of the Supreme Council for Islamic Revolution in Iraq (SCIRI). In a public sermon . . . al-Hakim, the head of the largest bloc in Parliament, advocated a Shiite provincial confederacy in the south that would unite eight or nine largely Shiite provinces into a federal region. He said that such loose federalism "does not spell partition." Addressing his followers at a mosque in Baghdad on the Eid al-Fitr, the celebration of the breaking of the Ramadan fast, al-Hakim said, "everyone should be reassured that we are supporters of the unity of Iraq and will stand against any plan for partition."

Al-Hakim went on, however, to condemn a strong central government as inherently tyrannical. He also pointed to history as support for his plan. He said that under the Ottoman Empire, Iraq had consisted of three big provinces, Mosul, Baghdad and Basra. What he did not say was that what is now Iraq was not a nation-state then but part of a large empire, and that even the Ottomans ruled Mosul and Basra through Baghdad. The three were not equal as provinces.

Iraqi Regional Governments

Al-Hakim's scheme for a southern Iraqi super-province, which some have called "Sumer," after the ancient civilization of southern Iraq, is vehemently opposed by the Sunni Arab minority, the recruitment pool for the former ruling elite. Sunni Arabs lack much in the way of petroleum or gas in the areas where they predominate, and they fear that the Shiites will monopolize the vast Rumaylah oil field and other fields yet to be discovered if they have their own semiautonomous region.

The young nationalist Shiite cleric Muqtada al-Sadr also rejects this plan in favor of a relatively strong central government. The wily al-Hakim, however, outmaneuvered both al-Sadr and the Sunnis in early October and rammed through Parliament a law authorizing the formation of the southern regional government. He scraped together a coalition of members of his own party, weaker factions of other Shiite parties, independents and Kurds to gain a bare majority of 140 out of 275 votes.

The Kurds supported al-Hakim, presumably because the creation of a Shiite regional government modeled on their Kurdistan (which groups Irbil, Dohuk and Sulaymaniyah) helps legitimate the idea of regional confederacies and protects Kurdish gains in greater self-determination. The Kurds

Iraq's Neighboring Countries

TAKEN FROM: CNN interactive, "Where Iraq's Neighbors Stand," 1997.
http://www.cnn.com/SPECIALS/1997/iraq/iraq.maps/neighbors/.

have been a prime mover in Iraq's march toward decentralization, and they probably would not mind much if the Sunnis and the Shiites did establish their own regions.

Iranian and Saudi Arabian Involvement

The biggest foreign backer of al-Hakim's scheme, meanwhile, is the Iranian regime. A southern Shiite "Sumer" region with partial or complete autonomy would inevitably, Iranian leaders believe, fall into the orbit of Shiite Iran. And that prospect is particularly alarming to the Saudis and the United States.

[In 2005], the *New York Times* quoted Saud al-Faisal, the Saudi foreign minister, saying that "the main worry of all the neighbors" was that the potential disintegration of Iraq into Sunni, Shiite and Kurdish states would "bring other countries in the region into the conflict." In particular, he worries about

Iran. He told the Council on Foreign Relations [in fall 2005], "We fought a war together to keep Iran out of Iraq after Iraq was driven out of Kuwait. Now we are handing the whole country over to Iran without reason." He was referring to the domination of Parliament and 11 of the country's provinces by Shiite fundamentalist parties, especially the Iran-backed SCIRI.

[In October 2006], with the possibility of partition becoming more likely, the Saudis attempted for the first time to intervene in the Iraq crisis in a major way. They, hosted a conference in Mecca of Sunni and Shiite clergymen from Iraq. In a historic achievement, the Saudis persuaded their guests to issue a joint fatwa, or religious legal ruling, that it is impermissible for a Muslim to shed the blood of another Muslim. They declared that the difference between Shiites and Sunnis was merely a matter of personal opinion and did not rise to the level of a dispute about first principles.

The Saudis hoped that, through this conference, they could begin a process whereby Sunni and Shiite reprisal killings in Iraq could be halted. The tit-for-tat sectarian violence is the main reason many Iraqis have begun taking the idea of partition seriously.

A War Extending Beyond Iraq's Borders

But aside from the selfish interests of all the political actors inside and outside Iraq, as a *practical* policy, partitioning Iraq is too risky. It would probably not reduce ethnic infighting. It might produce more. The mini-states that emerge from a partition will have plenty of reason to fight wars with one another, as India did with Pakistan in the 1940s and has done virtually ever since. Worse, it is likely that if the Sunni Arab mini-state commits an atrocity against the Shiites, it might well bring in the Iranian Revolutionary Guards. They in turn would be targeted by Saudi and Jordanian jihadi volunteers.

A break-up of Iraq might not stop at Iraq's borders. The Sunni Arabs could be picked up by Syria, thus greatly increasing Syria's fighting power. Or they could become a revolutionary force in Jordan. A wholesale renegotiation of national borders may ensue, according to some thinkers. Such profound changes in such a volatile part of the world cannot be depended on to occur without bloodshed. The region is already racked by the Arab-Israeli conflict and the struggle between secular and religious politics.

If Iraq does sink into long-term instability, it will not hold the world harmless. With two-thirds of the globe's proven petroleum reserves and 45 percent of its natural gas, the Persian Gulf hinterland of Iraq is key to the well-being of an industrialized or industrializing world. Long-term political instability in this region could drive petroleum prices so high as to endanger the world economy.

Ironically, those who plotted the Iraq war as a guarantee that the new century would also be an American one may well have put U.S. energy security in such question, and so weakened the dollar, as to raise the question of whether U.S. power has been dealt a permanent setback. Americans should pray that Iraqis heed the fatwa issued in Saudi Arabia late last week, forbidding inter-Muslim bloodshed.

| *"Those who argue for partition only exacerbate tensions."*

Partitioning Iraq Would Create Internal Instability

Jonathan Steele

In the following viewpoint, Jonathan Steele, a columnist and foreign correspondent for the The Guardian *newspaper in the United Kingdom, asserts that partitioning Iraq will lead to increased ethnic violence. According to Steele, drawing boundaries will force the relocation of thousands of vulnerable refugees and bring about artificial divisions in a country that has enjoyed a peaceful unity for decades. Steele believes the West should work on less radical means of stabilizing ethnic tensions before resorting to partition.*

As you read, consider the following questions:

1. As Steele suggests, why were Yezidi civilians targeted by al-Qaeda suicide bombers in mid-August 2007 massacres?

2. Who is Cyril Radcliffe and why does Steele refer to him in this viewpoint?

Jonathan Steele, "The Advocates of Partition in Iraq Only Make Things Worse," guardian.co.uk, August 24, 2007. Reproduced by permission of Guardian News Service, LTD.

3. Why does Steele believe that it is "too early to abandon hope that [ethnic tensions] can be reversed"?

The death toll from [mid-August 2007's] staggeringly brutal attacks by suicide bombers on two small-town communities in northern Iraq has crept up above 500, making it by far the worst atrocity since the 2003 invasion. No other mass killing has come within even half that total. Why did four truck bombers make these people their target? The mind struggles for an answer. The Yezidis are one of Iraq's smallest religious minorities, who follow an ancient cult unique to themselves. They wield no political or economic power. They live in an area that is remote from the key cities at the eye of Iraq's recurring hurricanes.

Yet there is a potential explanation for their killing, if such things can ever be explained. It carries a lesson for Iraq's future that goes much further than the tragedy of two marginal communities, and by coincidence has echoes in other events that occurred last week [August 2007]—the ceremonies marking 60 years since India's independence. The key word is partition, and the lesson is "Beware partition".

Ethnic Vengeance Killings

Most media coverage of the Yezidi massacre has concentrated on its religious dimension. Reporters pointed to the recent "honour killing" by a stone-throwing Yezidi mob of a young Yezidi girl who married a Muslim and apparently then converted to Islam. The killing was filmed and put on the Internet. Sunni Arab extremists linked to al-Qaida then took their anger out, it seems, against the whole Yezidi community.

But, as *The Guardian*'s Michael Howard pointed out, the ethnic dimension may be more important. Yezidis are Kurds and they live in areas that are being increasingly contested. According to Iraq's constitution, a referendum is supposed to be held there by the end of [2007] on whether to join the autonomous region of Kurdistan. Eliminating the Yezidis reduces the chances of the referendum going in favour of the Kurds.

Long before last week's atrocity, ethnic cleansing was under way elsewhere in Nineveh province and its capital city, Mosul. Like the British in Basra who have given up trying to stop intra-Shia strife, the Americans in Mosul have proved powerless to prevent that city's battle between Arabs and Kurds. The eastern half of the city and the adjacent Nineveh plains are Kurdish. The west is largely Arab, now the Yezidi are being intimidated to leave. Christian and Turcoman communities in the region look on anxiously, or flee. In Kirkuk, a contested city in one of Iraq's best oil regions, ethnic cleansing is also going on, albeit on a less dramatic scale.

Redrawing Borders Is Sparking Violence

It is a fair bet that if these various regions—which the Kurds claim as ancestral lands—were not threatened with frontier changes much of this violence would be reduced.

To the bureaucratic eye, partition seems a neat solution. But it often creates more problems than it solves. Where does the new borderline run, and who will be in charge of drawing it? In India Cyril Radcliffe, a British lawyer with no experience of the area, working largely with maps and consulting none of the affected people, carved up the subcontinent in less than five weeks [in 1947]. As he worked, ethnic cleansing and killing accelerated as Hindus, Sikhs and Muslims tried to show they were the majority in every multicultural district.

What happens to minorities who are "left behind" and find themselves outside the new entity where their group forms a majority? They are often "transferred" against their will, or forced to flee like the Hindus of Lahore. Some argue that without partition the killing in India would have been worse, and that the atrocities of 1947 and 1948 affected only a small percentage of the region's population. Independent India had then, and still has, more Muslim citizens than Paki-

War Within and Among Mini-States

Even if we could somehow partition Iraq—and no one has put forth a credible plan for splitting up multi-sectarian metropolises like Baghdad and Mosul—it is not at all clear that the resulting mini-states would be any more peaceful or stable than today's (nominally) unitary polity. At present, there is considerable turmoil in southern and western Iraq even though the former region is almost exclusively Shiite and the latter almost exclusively Sunni. We could expect even tougher struggles for power within individually constituted "Iraqistans," not to speak of war among the three mini-states themselves. To cite just one potential source of discord: absent some kind of ironclad outside guarantee, no Sunni state, lacking its own natural resources, could possibly trust a Shiite-dominated government to share its oil wealth equitably.

Max Boot, "How Not to Get Out of Iraq,"
Commentary, *September 2007.*

stan—eloquent proof that they live normally in a state that prides itself on its multi-ethnic, multi-religious identity.

Exacerbating Sectarian Tensions

Today's Iraq is very far from that. But this does not mean that it cannot one day revert to the multicultural tolerance it enjoyed in the pre-Saddam era. Sectarianism was deliberately cultivated by him on a "divide and repress" basis. The occupation forces then made the mistake of using sectarian and ethnic criteria for selecting the Iraqis they wanted as their postwar allies. Finally, attracted into Iraq by the chance to humiliate Americans as they were to Afghanistan against the

Russians two decades earlier, al-Qaida joined the mix by infiltrating Iraq and deliberately provoking sectarian violence through targeting Shia civilians with suicide bombs.

Grim though the result is, today's heightened ethnic and sectarian consciousness in Iraq's towns and cities is not a result of ancient hatreds. It is too early to abandon hope that it can be reversed, or that Iraq can one day be liberated from the interference of foreigners, whether they are western troops or Islamic jihadis.

Those who argue for partition only exacerbate tensions. Many Kurds want it, but it is not the dominant Shia or Sunni view. Surveys of attitudes in Iraq still show more Arabs define themselves as Iraqis than as Sunnis or Shias. To his credit, George [W.] Bush has not advocated partition, nor does it seem to be part of his hidden agenda. His remarks this week about Vietnam and what followed in Indochina after the US [United States] left, as well as his refusal to contemplate any withdrawal from Iraq while he remains president, were misguided and dangerous. At least he has not come out for splitting the country.

It is the Democrats who seem more tempted by it. Hillary Clinton [Senator, D-New York] has suggested keeping a substantial US force in Kurdistan if troops pull out of Baghdad and the south. So have Senator Joe Biden [D-Delaware], another presidential candidate [2008], and Richard Holbrooke, the former ambassador to the UN [United Nations]. They may be arguing this as a way of minimising the image of humiliation and retreat when the US eventually has to give up its foolish Iraqi venture. But it is wrong.

Stability First

Meanwhile the deadline for the referendum on Kirkuk and the other contested regions in the north approaches. The priority must be to put it off until Iraq reaches some form of stability. It will be a bitter blow to the Kurdish political parties who have staked so much on it, but they will not risk violence in opposing a postponement. They have thrived in showing the world they can run their own region responsibly. Let them be satisfied with what they have, and not insist on having more just now.

"We refuse the resolutions that decide
Iraq's destiny from outside Iraq."

Iraqis Reject U.S. Partitioning Plans

Ned Parker and Raheem Salman

In the following viewpoint, Ned Parker and Raheem Salman reveal the opinions of a few Iraqi leaders concerning the U.S.-proposed partition of Iraq along sectarian and ethnic lines. As Parker and Salman report, Iraqi spokespersons from Shiite and Sunni political factions reject foreign intervention in shaping the future of Iraq and are supporting a stronger national government as opposed to a collection of weaker regional governments run by Shiite, Sunni, and Kurdish blocs. Ned Parker is a Baghdad correspondent for the Los Angeles Times *and Raheem Salman is a staff writer for the newspaper.*

As you read, consider the following questions:

1. According to the quoted statement signed by Sunni and Shiite political blocs, how did these Iraqis interpret the long-term plans of the U.S. Congress when it passed the decentralization resolution in September 2007?

2. What two foreign powers do the authors say have occupied Iraq in times prior to the U.S. invasion?

3. According to Parker and Salman, how did the U.S. Embassy in Iraq react to Congress's call to decentralize Iraq?

Iraq's political leadership, in a rare show of unity, skewered a nonbinding U.S. Senate resolution passed [in September 2007] that endorses the decentralization of Iraq through the establishment of semiautonomous regions.

The measure, which calls for a relatively weak central government and strong regional authorities in Sunni Arab, Shiite and Kurdish areas, has touched a nerve here, raising fears that the United States is planning to partition Iraq.

"The Congress adopted this proposal based on an incorrect reading and unrealistic estimations of the history, present and future of Iraq," said Izzat Shahbandar, a member of former interim Prime Minister Iyad Allawi's secular parliamentary bloc.

He was reading from a statement also signed by preeminent Shiite Muslim religious parties and the main Sunni Arab bloc.

"It represents a dangerous precedent to establishing the nature of the relationship between Iraq and the U.S.A.," the statement said, "and shows the Congress as if it were planning for a long-term occupation by their country's troops."

Rejecting Foreign Plans to Shape Iraq

The nonbinding measure was approved in Washington on Wednesday [, September 26, 2007,] and resentment appears to be building daily in Iraq. Passed by senators, 75 to 23, it supports a "federal system" that would create regions dominated by sect and ethnicity.

The measure was sponsored by Sen. Joseph R. Biden Jr. of Delaware, a Democratic candidate for president. Biden, along with Council of Foreign Relations president emeritus Leslie Gelb, has advocated that the country be divided up along ethnic, sectarian and regional lines.

Northern Iraq already has a semiautonomous region ruled by Kurds, but its leaders want to annex adjacent areas with dominant Kurdish populations.

The federalization idea, backed by some Democrats, is one of many proposals floated in the U.S., where the public has become disillusioned with the continuing violence in Iraq.

But the Senate resolution, whatever its intended effect, has backfired in Baghdad, where it has been interpreted in light of Iraq's history of foreign occupation, from the Ottoman Empire to Britain and now the United States. Iraqi political parties that have been deadlocked for months on issues such as a national oil law have rallied to defend the country's sovereignty and to repulse any effort by another country to shape Iraq's fate.

"We refuse the resolutions that decide Iraq's destiny from outside Iraq. This is a dangerous partitioning based on sectarianism and ethnicity," said Hashim Taie, a member of the Iraqi Accordance Front, the parliament's main Sunni bloc.

Shiite cleric Muqtada Sadr's political supporters joined their Shiite rivals in denouncing the Senate's measure. "This project is the strategic option for the American administration in its failure to ignite a sectarian war inside Iraq," Nassar Rubaie said. "They started to search for a replacement, which is to divide Iraq."

Senate Plan Plays on Iraqi Fears

Federalism has long proved a charged topic for Iraq. The Sadr loyalists have sought a strong national government. The Supreme Islamic Iraqi Council, another large Shiite political faction, has also started to discourage the idea of further weakening an already frail government.

Opposition in Iraq

Iraq's dominant political parties blasted the resolution [calling for partition] as "a threat to Iraq sovereignty and unity ... based on an incorrect reading and unrealistic estimations of the history, present and future of Iraq." In a statement signed by the leading Shi'ite, Sunni and secular blocs in the Iraqi parliament, these elected political leaders argued that "It represents a dangerous precedent to establishing the nature of the relationship between Iraq and the U.S.A. and shows the Congress as if it were planning for a long-term occupation by their country's troops."

Furthermore, polls have shown a clear majority of Iraqis support national unity and a strong central government.

Even the U.S. State Department found the Senate resolution too extreme. "As we have said in the past, attempts to partition or divide Iraq by intimidation, force or other means into three separate states would produce extraordinary suffering and bloodshed," read a statement from the U.S. Embassy in Baghdad, adding that, "the United States has made clear our strong opposition to such attempts" and "partition is not on the table."

Stephen Zunes, "Support for Iraq Partition: Cynical and Dangerous," October 12, 2007. www.fpif.org.

Leery of American intervention, Rubaie said the powers of the provinces and regional blocs should be defined once the U.S. withdraws from Iraq.

The U.S. Embassy in Baghdad was quick to issue a statement Sunday distancing itself from the Democrat-led Senate.

Joost Hiltermann, a Middle East expert at the International Crisis Group think tank, said the Senate proposal had roused some of the worst fears of Arab states. "In Iraq and the Arab world, the word 'partition' is an anathema associated with the worst aspects of imperialist policy," he said.

Periodical Bibliography

The following articles have been selected to supplement the diverse views presented in this chapter.

Fouad Ajami "The Great Circle of Enmity," *U.S. News & World Report*, May 21, 2007.

Ed Blanche "Dividing Iraq," *Middle East*, November 2007.

Borzou Daragahi "Shiites Press for a Partition of Iraq," *Los Angeles Times*, August 9, 2006.

Babak Dehghanpisheh "A Civil War on Campus," *Newsweek*, November 12, 2007.

Robert Dreyfuss "Is There a Nationalist Solution in Iraq?" *American Prospect*, June 5, 2007. www.prospect.org.

Abigail Hauslohner "Reconciliation at Iraq's Ground Zero," *Time*, August 6, 2008.

Ellen Knickmeyer "Sectarian Strife in Iraq Imperils Entire Region, Analysts Warn," *Washington Post*, November 16, 2006.

Charles Krauthammer "The Partitioning of Iraq," *Washington Post*, September 7, 2007.

Mark Kukis "Dark Days for Iraq's Awakening," *Time*, September 1, 2008.

Noam N. Levey "Senate Backs Separating Iraq into Three Regions," *Los Angeles Times*, September 27, 2007.

Timothy Noah "Kurd Sellout Watch, Day 421: Should We Partition Iraq?" April 27, 2004. www.slate.com.

OPPOSING
VIEWPOINTS®
SERIES

CHAPTER 3

What Should U.S. Policy Be Toward a Post-War Iraq?

Chapter Preface

On November 26, 2007, President George W. Bush, Iraq's Prime Minister Nouri al-Maliki, and other Iraqi leaders signed the Declaration of Principles for Friendship and Cooperation between Iraq and the United States. This non-binding agreement is ostensibly an agenda for how the two nations will formalize bilateral relations in the immediate future—when the presidential term of the Bush administration has come to an end. Speaking of the agreement, Bush stated that Iraq's leaders "understand that their success will require U.S. political, economic, and security engagement that extends beyond my presidency. These Iraqi leaders have asked for an enduring relationship with America."

The declaration anticipates that the United States will extend support to the new Iraqi government in three main venues: the political and diplomatic sphere, the economic arena, and national defense. In offering political aid, America is called upon to assist in national reconciliation among Iraq's various religious and ethnic sects and to work with other states in the region to resolve "outstanding problems." As for economic support, the United States pledges to help rebuild Iraq's markets and industries with both financial and technical support and normalize trade relations between Iraq and global markets.

The final section of the agreement has been the most controversial. It stipulates that the United States will provide "security assurances and commitments to the Republic of Iraq to deter foreign aggression" and support "the Republic of Iraq in its efforts to combat all terrorist groups . . . and destroy their logistical networks and their sources of finance, and defeat and uproot them from Iraq." Critics of the agreement are concerned that these guidelines suggest an unquestioned sanction for the continued involvement of U.S. troops in Iraq for an unspecified length of time. Indeed, Iraqi officials are quoted as saying that their country expects that 50,000 U.S. troops (down from the present 160,000) will be tolerated in Iraq for an undisclosed period of time in exchange for the declaration's security assurances.

Congressional leaders are also worried that the Declaration of Principles might be an illegal military treaty in disguise. After all, the President is commonly required to seek congressional approval to involve U.S. troops in military actions and to secure federal funds to pay for such ventures. Representative William D. Delahunt of Massachusetts, chairman of a foreign affairs subcommittee that debated the Declaration of Principles, has argued that Congress should be involved in ratifying such a wide-ranging agreement. "It is my position," he said, "that the American people have a right to be fully and directly informed as to the intentions of the administration regarding any agreement with the Government of Iraq. The American people have paid dearly for that right, almost 4,000 of our sons and daughters have died in that conflict, and tens of thousands have been seriously injured." Still, the administration has denied that the agreement is anything but a road map of future relations; Secretary of Defense Robert Gates even stated that the United States was not intending to propose a mutual defense agreement—though the text of the Declaration of Principles suggests otherwise.

In the following chapter, Lawrence J. Korb takes up Representative Delahunt's concern while other commentators discuss and debate just what America's policy toward Iraq should be in the coming years.

"The United States needs to adopt a withdrawal strategy measured in months, not years. . . . A longer schedule would simply prolong the agony."

The United States Should Withdraw Its Troops from Iraq

Ted Galen Carpenter

In the following viewpoint, Ted Galen Carpenter argues that the United States must withdraw its troops from Iraq. In Carpenter's view, keeping American troops in Iraq is too expensive, strains the effectiveness of the military, and damages America's credibility in the global community. He acknowledges that leaving will be difficult, but he insists that the United States can only salvage its reputation and cut its human and economic costs by pulling out of Iraq immediately. Ted Galen Carpenter is the vice president of Defense and Foreign Policy Studies at the Cato Institute, a libertarian public policy research organization.

Ted Galen Carpenter, "Escaping the Trap: Why the United States Must Leave Iraq," Ted Galen Carpenter's Statement before the Senate Foreign Relations Committee, January 11, 2007. Republished with permission of The Cato Institute, conveyed through Copyright Clearance Center, Inc.

As you read, consider the following questions:

1. What does Carpenter give as the range of U.S. soldier deployments needed to successfully suppress violence in Iraq?

2. How does Carpenter refute the claim that leaving Iraq would be immoral?

3. How has the occupation of Iraq diluted the standards of military recruitment, according to Carpenter?

Optimism about the U.S. mission in Iraq has faded dramatically [at the end of 2006]. The bipartisan Iraq Study group conceded that the situation in Iraq was "grave and deteriorating." The Pentagon's report to Congress in November 2006 paints a similarly dismal picture, with attacks on U.S. troops, Iraqi security forces, and Iraqi civilians at record levels.

Yet proponents of the war refuse to admit what is becoming increasingly obvious: Washington's Iraq occupation and democratization mission is failing, and there is little realistic prospect that its fortunes will improve. Something much more dramatic than a modest course correction is needed.

It is essential to ask the administration and its hawkish backers at what point they will admit that the costs of this venture have become unbearable. How much longer are they willing to have our troops stay in Iraq? Five years? Ten years? Twenty years? How many more tax dollars are they willing to pour into Iraq? Another $300 billion? $600 billion? $1 trillion? And most crucial of all, how many more American lives are they willing to sacrifice? Two thousand? Five thousand? Ten thousand? Proponents of the mission avoid addressing such unpleasant questions. Instead, they act as though victory in Iraq can be achieved merely through the exercise of will power.

The Dire Security Situation in Iraq

Whether or not one describes it as a civil war, the security situation in Iraq is extraordinarily violent and chaotic. Moreover, the nature of the violence in that country has shifted since the February 2006 bombing of the Golden Mosque in Samarra, one of Shia Islam's holiest sites. The Sunni-led insurgency against U.S. and British occupation forces and the security forces of the U.S.-sponsored Iraqi government is still a significant factor, but it is no longer the dominant one. The turmoil now centers around sectarian violence between Sunnis and Shiites. Baghdad is the epicenter of that strife, but it has erupted in other parts of the country as well. The Iraq Study Group noted that four of Iraq's 18 provinces are "highly insecure." Those provinces account for about 40 percent of the country's population.

A November 2006 UN [United Nations] report highlights the extent of the growing bloodshed. The carnage is now running at approximately 120 victims each day. This is occurring in a country of barely 26 million people. A comparable pace in the United States would be a horrifying 1,400 deaths per day—or nearly 500,000 per year. If violence between feuding political or ethno-religious factions was consuming that many American lives, there would be little debate about whether the United States was experiencing a civil war.

In addition to the casualties in Iraq, there are other human costs. The United Nations estimates that some 1.6 million people have been displaced inside Iraq (i.e., they are "internal refugees") as a result of the fighting. Another 1.8 million have fled the country entirely, mostly to Jordan and Syria. Moreover, the pace of the exodus is accelerating. Refugees are now leaving Iraq at the rate of nearly 3,000 a day. The bulk of those refugees are middle and upper class families. Indeed, there are affluent neighborhoods in Baghdad and other cities that now resemble ghost towns.

The Complex Nature of the Violence

The mounting chaos in Iraq is not simply a case of Sunni-Shiite sectarian violence, although that is the dominant theme.

The Iraq Study Group notes the complexity of Iraq's security turmoil. "In Kirkuk, the struggle is between Kurds, Arabs, and Turkmen. In Basra and the south, the violence is largely an intra-Shia struggle." Implicitly rejecting the arguments of those who contend that the violence is primarily a Sunni-Shia conflict confined to Baghdad, the members of the commission point out that "most of Iraq's cities have a sectarian mix and are plagued by persistent violence." Prime Minister Nouri al-Maliki warns that conflicts in the various regions could be "Shi'ite versus Shi'ite and Sunni versus Sunni."

There is also mounting evidence that the majority of Iraqis no longer want U.S. troops in their country. The bottom line is that the United States is mired in a country that is already in the early stages of an exceedingly complex, multi-sided civil war, and where all significant factions save one (the Kurds) want American troops to leave. That is an untenable situation.

Illusory Solution—Send More Troops

Increasing the number of U.S. troops in Iraq by 20,000 or so is a futile attempt to salvage a mission that has gone terribly wrong. In all likelihood, it would merely increase the number of casualties—both American and Iraqi—over the short term while having little long-term impact on the security environment. Moreover, the magnitude of the proposed buildup falls far short of the numbers needed to give the occupation forces a realistic prospect of suppressing the violence. Experts on counterinsurgency strategies have consistently concluded that at least 10 soldiers per 1,000 population are required to have a sufficient impact. Indeed, some experts have argued that in cases where armed resistance is intense and pervasive (which certainly seems to apply to Iraq), deployments of 20 soldiers per thousand may be needed.

Given Iraq's population (26 million) such a mission would require the deployment of at least 260,000 ground forces (an increase of 115,000 from current levels) and probably as many as 520,000. Even the lower requirement will strain the U.S. Army and Marine Corps to the breaking point. Yet a lesser deployment would have no realistic chance to get the job done. A limited "surge" of additional troops is the latest illusory panacea [remedy] offered by the people who brought us the Iraq quagmire [predicament] in the first place. It is an idea that should be rejected.

Consequences of Leaving

Proponents of staying in Iraq offer several reasons why a prompt withdrawal would be bad for the United States. Those arguments vary in terms of plausibility. All of them, though, are ultimately deficient as a reason for keeping U.S. troops in Iraq.

Al-Qaeda Would Not Take Over Iraq

Administration officials and other supporters of the war have warned repeatedly that a "premature" withdrawal of U.S. forces would enable Al-Qaeda to turn Iraq into a sanctuary to plot and launch attacks against the United States and other Western countries. But Al-Qaeda taking over Iraq is an extremely improbable scenario. The Iraq Study Group put the figure of foreign fighters at only 1,300, a relatively small component of the Sunni insurgency against U.S. forces. It strains credulity to imagine 1,300 fighters (and foreigners at that) taking over and controlling a country of 26 million people.

The challenge for Al-Qaeda would be even more daunting than those raw numbers suggest. The organization does have some support among the Sunni Arabs in Iraq, but opinion even among that segment of the population is divided. A September 2006 poll conducted by the Program on International Policy Attitudes [PIPA] at the University of Maryland found that 94 percent of Sunnis had a somewhat or highly unfavorable attitude toward Al-Qaeda. As the violence of Al-Qaeda attacks has mounted, and the victims are increasingly Iraqis, not Americans, many Sunnis have turned against the terrorists. There have even been a growing number of reports during the past year of armed conflicts between Iraqi Sunnis and foreign fighters.

The PIPA poll also showed that 98 percent of Shiite respondents and 100 percent of Kurdish respondents had somewhat or very unfavorable views of Al-Qaeda. The notion that a Shiite-Kurdish-dominated government would tolerate Iraq becoming a safe haven for Al-Qaeda is improbable on its face. And even if U.S. troops left Iraq, the successor government would continue to be dominated by the Kurds and Shiites, since they make up more than 80 percent of Iraq's population and, in marked contrast to the situation under Saddam Hussein, they now control the military and police. That doesn't suggest a reliable safe haven for Al-Qaeda.

The Terrorists Would Not Be Emboldened Worldwide

In urging the United States to persevere in Iraq, President [George W.] Bush has warned that an early military withdrawal would encourage Al-Qaeda and other terrorist organizations. Weak U.S. responses to challenges over the previous quarter century, especially in Lebanon and Somalia, had emboldened such people, Bush argues. Hawkish pundits have made similar allegations.

It is a curious line of argument with ominous implications, for it assumes that the United States should have stayed in both countries, despite the military debacles there. The mistake, according to that logic, was not the original decision to intervene but the decision to limit American losses and terminate the missions. That is a classic case of learning the wrong lessons from history.

Yes, Al-Qaeda and other terrorist groups apparently concluded that the Lebanon and Somalia episodes showed that

U.S. leaders and the American people have no stomach for enduring murky missions that entail significant casualties. They are likely to draw a similar lesson if the United States withdraws from Iraq without an irrefutable triumph. That is why it is so imperative to be cautious about a decision to intervene in the first place. Military missions should not be undertaken unless there are indisputably vital American security interests at stake. . . .

Leaving Iraq Would Not Betray a Moral Obligation to the Iraqi People

In addition to their other objections, opponents of withdrawal protest that we will leave Iraq in chaos, and that would be an immoral action on the part of the United States. Even some critics of the war have been susceptible to that argument, invoking the so-called Pottery Barn principle: "You broke it, you bought it."

There are two major problems with that argument. First, unless some restrictions are put in place, the obligation is seemingly open-ended. There is little question that chaos might increase in Iraq after U.S. forces leave, but advocates of staying the course do not explain how the United States can prevent the contending factions in Iraq from fighting the civil war they already seem to have started. At least, no one has explained how the United States can restore the peace there as anything resembling a reasonable cost in American blood and treasure.

Leaving aside the very real possibility that the job of building a stable democracy might never be done, the moral obligation thesis begs a fundamental question: What about the moral obligation of the U.S. government to its own soldiers and to the American people? There is clearly an obligation not to waste either American lives [or] American tax dollars. We are doing both in Iraq. Staying the course is not a moral strategy; it is the epitome of an immoral one.

A Phased Withdrawal of U.S. Troops

When the new administration takes office in January 2009, it must [begin a phased withdrawal] by initiating a down payment on redeployment. Starting from the roughly 15 combat brigades (a total of 130,000–140,000 troops) it is likely to inherit, the new administration should signal its intention to transition to a "support," or "overwatch," role by announcing the near-term reduction of U.S. forces to perhaps 12 brigades. The new administration should also immediately sign a formal pledge with the Iraqi government stating unequivocally that it will not seek, accept, or under any conditions establish permanent or "enduring" military bases in Iraq. Taken together, these actions would signal to the Iraqi government that the U.S. commitment is no longer open-ended while still maintaining enough forces in the near term to prevent a major reversal of progress on security. These steps would also signal to groups inside the Iraqi parliament that strongly oppose the occupation (especially the Sadrists), as well as to the organizations representing the nationalist wing of the Sunni insurgency, that the United States does not intend to stay forever.

Colin H. Kahl and William E. Odom, "When to Leave Iraq,"
Foreign Affairs, *July-August 2008.*

The Consequences of Staying in Iraq

Leaving Iraq is clearly not cost-free, but the costs (both tangible and intangible) of a prompt exit must be measured against the costs of staying the course. Moreover, even if the United States absorbs the costs of a prolonged mission, there is no certainty that anything resembling victory resides at the end of that effort. Indeed, most of the indicators suggest that we would be merely delaying defeat.

Damage to America's Standing in the World

Even the September 2006 National Intelligence Estimate on Iraq conceded that the U.S. occupation of Iraq had served as a focal point and inspiration for Muslim extremists. Equally worrisome, it had also served as a training arena for such militants to hone their military and terrorist skills. An Al-Qaeda letter intercepted by the U.S. military indicates that the organization itself regards a continued U.S. military presence and, consequently, a long war in Iraq as a boon to its cause.

A December 2006 Zogby poll of populations in five Arab nations reveals just how much anti-U.S. sentiment has increased throughout that region. Opinions of the United States, which were already rather negative, have grown significantly worse in the past year.

Outside the Arab world, there also has been a hardening of attitudes toward the United States. Even among long-standing friends and allies (in such places as Europe and East Asia), the United States is viewed in a significantly more negative light. The longer we stay in Iraq, the worse those problems will become.

Straining the All-Volunteer Military

Even some hawks are concerned about the negative impact of the Iraq mission on the all-volunteer force (AVF). They should be concerned. In December 2006, Gen. Peter J. Schoomaker, the Army's chief of staff, bluntly told a House committee that the active-duty Army "will break" unless there was a permanent increase in force structure. And that is before any contemplated additional deployments to Iraq.

The military leaders are not exaggerating. Already the Army has struggled to meet its recruiting goals, even though it has diluted the standards for new recruits, including by issuing waivers in cases where there is evidence of criminal behavior or mental illness. Indeed, the Iraq occupation has been sustained to this point only through extraordinary exertions, including an unprecedented number of "stop loss" orders, preventing military personnel from returning to civilian life when their terms of enlistment are up, and recalling members of the reserves—including some people in their 40s and 50s. The AVF is straining to the breaking point already, and the longer we stay in Iraq, the worse those strains will become.

Costs in Blood and Treasure

The tab for the Iraq mission is already more than $350 billion, and the meter is now running at approximately $8 billion a month. Furthermore, even those appalling figures do not take into account indirect costs, such as long-term care for wounded Iraq war veterans.

Except when the survival of the nation is at stake, all military missions must be judged according to a cost-benefit calculation. Iraq has never come close to being a war for America's survival. Even the connection of the Iraq mission to the larger war against radical Islamic terrorism was always tenuous, at best. For all of his odious qualities, [Iraq's former ruler] Saddam Hussein was a secular tyrant, not an Islamic radical. Indeed, the radical Islamists expressed nearly as much hatred for Saddam as they did for the United States. Iraq was an elective war—a war of choice, and a bad choice at that.

Deciding to Leave

The United States needs to adopt a withdrawal strategy measured in months, not years. Indeed, the president should begin the process of removing American troops immediately, and that process needs to be complete in no more than six months. A longer schedule would simply prolong the agony. It would also afford various Iraq factions (especially the Kurds and some of the Shia political players) the opportunity to try to entice or manipulate the United States into delaying the withdrawal of its forces still further.

Emotionally, deciding to leave under current conditions will not be easy, for it requires an implicit admission that Washington has failed in its ambitious goal to create a stable, united, democratic, secular Iraq that would be a model for peace throughout the Middle East. But that goal was unrealistic from the outset. It is difficult for any nation, and especially the American superpower, to admit failure. However, it is better to admit failure when the adverse consequences are relatively modest. A defeat in Iraq would assuredly be a setback for the United States, particularly in terms of global clout and credibility. But one of the advantages to being a superpower is that the country can absorb a setback without experiencing catastrophic damage to its core interests or capabilities. Defeat in Iraq does not even come close to threatening those interests or capabilities. Most important, a withdrawal now will be less painful than withdrawing years from now when the cost in blood, treasure, and credibility will prove far greater.

> "The people of America need to understand this: the enemies of a stable Iraq are America's enemies, and they simply do not understand the language of civilization and reason."

The United States Should Keep Its Troops in Iraq

Part I: Erik Swabb; Part II: Mohammed Fadhil

In part I of the following viewpoint, Erik Swabb, a former U.S. Marine officer, contends that the United States should keep its troops in Iraq to secure it from insurgents. Swabb claims that the new strategy of stationing U.S. and Iraqi military units in cities—instead of at remote bases—is making the civilian population feel more secure and is cutting civilian ties to terrorists. In part II of the viewpoint, Mohammed Fadhil, an Iraqi dentist living in Baghdad, supports this view. He maintains that U.S. troops are needed to destroy terrorist cells and keep foreign powers such as Iran and Syria from casting their influence over an unstable Iraq.

Part I: Erik Swabb, "The U.S. Needs to Stay in Iraq," Boston.com, March 20, 2007. Reproduced by permission of Pars International. Part II: Mohammed Fadhil, "A Baghdad Plea: U.S. Should Stay and Fight," *Daily News*, May 10, 2007. Reproduced by permission.

As you read, consider the following questions:

1. How does Swabb refute the argument that pulling U.S. troops out of Iraq would benefit Iraqi security?

2. What has improved for U.S. forces after implementing the strategy of deploying troops in Iraq's towns and cities?

3. Who does Fadhil say is looking to control Iraq's people and wealth?

As the war in Iraq enters its fifth year [2007] with no end in sight, the public's desire to leave Iraq is understandable. But it is also unfortunate. The troop "surge" and the accompanying new security plan for Baghdad stand a real chance of reducing violence to a level that will allow the Iraqi government to emerge as a legitimate authority worth supporting. For the first time, the military is applying a winning strategy in the capital.

The central goal of fighting an insurgency is securing the population. Doing so drives a wedge between insurgents and the people among whom they hide and derive support.

Insurgents cannot operate if civilians consistently inform on their activities and refuse to harbor them. People are only willing to do so if they feel secure. Typically, this means a large, continual security presence among the people. Only then can economic development follow and finally win over the populace.

The Presence of Coalition Forces Quells Violence

Instead of this approach, top commanders in Iraq previously focused on the assumption that the presence of US [United States] troops fueled the insurgency. The goal was thus to replace US troops with Iraqi forces. As US troops left, security would improve. While this approach had a certain logic to it, facts on the ground never bore it out because Iraqi forces proved incapable or unwilling to protect both Sunnis and Shi'ites. Previous security plans for Baghdad consisted almost wholly of Iraqi forces and were complete failures.

The resulting chaos in Baghdad served as a wake-up call to the United States. The military adopted a bold new strategy, whose departure from the past has not been appreciated. Coalition forces are now committed to securing the population in Baghdad, not just turning over the fight to Iraqis. It is hard not to overstate the importance of the shift since it finally directs coalition efforts at the right objective.

The most important feature of the new strategy is joint security stations. The outposts are manpower intensive, which is why the troop surge is needed. A US unit is paired with an Iraqi counterpart and permanently stationed in residential areas.

This joint presence, which reduces abuse by Iraqi forces, protects Sunnis and Shi'itas, removing the impetus to resort to sectarian violence. The joint security stations have their critics. Some say they are easy stationary targets and will only increase US casualties. However, where a similar strategy has been employed, it has met with great success.

After the battles in Fallujah in November 2004, my commander had the wisdom to forward deploy our company in Iraqi towns and pair our platoons with Iraqi counterparts. It was no longer necessary to use vehicles to patrol from distant, large bases. Off the roads, we stopped suffering casualties from improvised explosive devices. Since we lived where we patrolled, we built trust with local Iraqis, which proved the catalyst for a wave of intelligence on insurgent activity.

The final result was no coalition casualties and an end to insurgent attacks in the area. Other units in Anbar Province have recently pursued a similar strategy and achieved success in securing cities along the Euphrates River, which serve as a supply line to Sunni insurgents in Baghdad. Apparently, most Iraqis care more about security than they do about the presence of US forces.

The Best Hope for a Secure Iraq

The joint security station concept would founder without the proper leadership to believe in it, promote it, and sustain it. Fortunately, such leadership is now in place. General David Petraeus, the new commander of US forces in Iraq, leads a dream team of the top specialists in counterinsurgency. While slow to come around, the US military is getting better at this complicated type of warfare.

The insurgents, of course, have a say in how the new plan unfolds. Violence has flared in nearby regions as insurgents flee Baghdad. Coalition forces thus must have enough time to develop the local relationships and intelligence needed to counter changing insurgent tactics. Recent calls by military commanders to maintain increased troop levels into 2008 reflect this reality.

The biggest danger now is that the public and Congress are so pessimistic that US forces will be withdrawn before the strategy has time to produce results. Ultimately, this view reflects a lack of understanding about how this strategy, unlike previous failed plans, is a real change in the right direction. Such skepticism is understandable considering the difficult last four years. But it risks cutting short the best hope yet for putting Iraq on the right course.

I wasn't surprised when I saw Al Qaeda's second-in-command, Ayman al-Zawahiri, appear on AI Jazeera to announce America's defeat [in May 2007], not long after U.S. Senate Majority Leader Harry Reid did. Zawahiri claims Al Qaeda has won, and Reid claims America has lost.

But from here in Baghdad, I see only a war that's still raging—with no victory in sight for Al Qaeda or any other entity. In fact, I see Al Qaeda on the ropes, losing support among my fellow Iraqis.

In the midst of such a fierce war, sending more wrong messages could only further complicate an already complicated situation. It would only create more of a mess inside

Opposition to Iraq War Is Divided After 5 Years

Does the United States have an obligation to establish a reasonable level of stability and security in Iraq before withdrawing all of its troops?

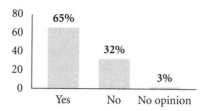

Are each of these developments more likely to occur if the United States keeps its troops in Iraq or withdraws its troops from Iraq?

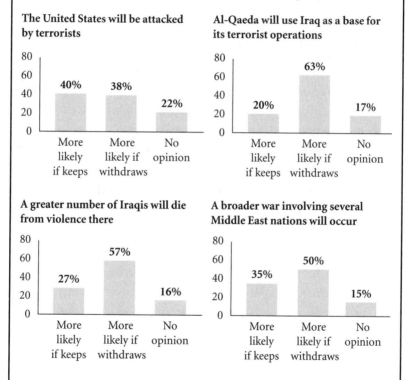

TAKEN FROM: USA Today/Gallup Poll of 2,021 Adults, February 21–24, 2008.

Iraq—a mess that would then be exploited by Iran, Syria and Saudi Arabia for their own purposes: more iron-fisted control of the peoples and treasures of the region, more pushing the Middle East to crises and confrontations, and more spreading of their dark, backward ideologies.

And so, as an Iraqi, I say without hesitation: the American forces should stay here, and further reinforcements should be sent if the situation requires them. Not only that, these forces should be prepared to expand their operations whenever and wherever necessary to strike hard at the nests of evil that not only threaten Iraq and the Middle East, but seek to blackmail the whole world in the ugliest way through pursuing nuclear weapons.

The Enemy Must Leave Iraq First

It is up to us to show tyrants and murderers like Iran's Mahmoud Ahmadinejad, Hezbollah's Hassan Nasrallah, Syria's Bashar Assad, and their would-be imitators who seek to control Iraq's people and wealth that we, the people, are not their possessions. They can't take out our humanity and they can't force us to back down.

The world should ask them to leave our land before asking the soldiers of freedom to do so.

The cost of liberating Europe in the last century was enormous in blood and treasure. In fact, it took half a century of American military presence thereafter to protect those nations from subsequent threats. If that made sense during a Cold War, and it did, then I don't understand why anyone would demand a pullout from Iraq (and maybe later, the entire Middle East) when the enemies are using every evil technique, from booby trapped dead animals to hijacked civilian aircrafts, to kill innocents.

And so, my friends, I will call for fighting this war just as powerfully as the bad guys do—because I must show them that I'm stronger than they are. The people of America need to understand this: the enemies of a stable Iraq are America's enemies, and they simply do not understand the language of civilization and reason.

They understand only power. It is with power they took over their countries and held their peoples hostage. Everything they accomplished was through absolute control over the assets of their nations through murder, torture, repression and intimidation.

Iraq Will Prevail with U.S. Help

Those who prefer to bury their heads in the dirt today, and withdraw from this difficult fight, will be cursed forever for abandoning their duty when they were most capable. I don't understand why someone who has all the tools for victory would refuse to fight an enemy that reminds us every day that it is evil—with all the daily beheadings, torture and violations of all humane laws and values.

With America's help—and only with its help—the decent people of Iraq can still prevail.

"Iraq's best chance for long-term stability is to develop democratic institutions that will protect the basic civil, political, and human liberties and rights of the Iraqi people."

The United States Should Promote Democracy in Iraq

Steven Groves

In the viewpoint that follows, Steven Groves contends that the work of the U.S. government and various non-governmental organizations in promoting democracy in Iraq is helping create a civil society there. Groves suggests that generating voter participation, instituting government accountability, and promoting civil and human rights in Iraq will undue years of political repression and bring forth democracy. He insists that the U.S. government must stay committed to this goal or risk continual anarchy in Iraq. Steven Groves is a fellow at the Kathryn and Shelby Cullom David Institute for International Studies, which is part of the Heritage Foundation, a conservative public policy think tank.

Steven Groves, "Advancing Freedom in Iraq," *Backgrounder*, July 30, 2007, pp. 1–4. Copyright © 2007 The Heritage Foundation. Reproduced by permission.

As you read, consider the following questions:

1. What does Groves say the National Democratic Institute for International Affairs is doing to promote democracy in Iraq?

2. What are CAPs and how do they function in Iraq, according to Groves?

3. What does Groves predict will happen if the United States withdraws its troops prematurely from Iraq?

Helping Iraq to become a secure and stable nation in the heart of the Middle East is in the national interest of the United States. Iraq's best chance for long-term stability is to develop democratic institutions that will protect the basic civil, political, and human liberties and rights of the Iraqi people.

In Iraq, freedom, democracy, and civil society—nonexistent under [former Iraqi leader] Saddam Hussein—remain precarious. U.S. government efforts, as well as the efforts of non-governmental organizations, to promote democracy and good governance rely on the security umbrella provided by the U.S. military presence. A precipitous U.S. military withdrawal would almost certainly doom U.S. and Iraqi efforts to build a free and democratic Iraq.

The Shiites, Sunnis, Kurds, and other factions require a secure environment to reach political accommodation. The United States and the international community should do everything possible to help to stabilize Iraq. Specifically, the U.S. Congress should not interfere with ongoing military efforts to secure and stabilize Iraq or legislate restrictions on the use of U.S. military force. . . .

Promoting Freedom and Democracy After Saddam

Promoting freedom and democracy in a country in which civil society has been pulverized by decades of brutal dictatorship is not easy. Over the past several years, Iraq has successfully held a series of nationwide elections for interim and permanent governments.

But while free and fair elections are a crucial component of democratic government, democracies require more than regularly held elections to remain viable. Elections alone will not guarantee that a sustainable and pluralistic polity will take root in Iraq. Iraq needs a robust civil society to ensure that its nascent democracy protects its citizens regardless of their political beliefs, respects the rights of women, and treats ethnic and religious minorities equally.

Civil society is composed of voluntary civic, social, and political organizations and institutions that form the basis of a functioning society, as opposed to government structures and the business community. These organizations and institutions serve as intermediaries between the government and the governed. Developing a robust civil society in Iraq would facilitate political awareness and create a more informed citizenry that would in turn make better voting choices, participate in politics, and hold the government accountable for its decisions. A healthy civil society is the backbone of a mature democracy.

Since the end of major combat operations, the United States has been working with Iraqi citizens to build democratic institutions and strengthen civil society through the U.S. Department of State, the U.S. Agency for International Development, and various non-governmental organizations (NGOs). These efforts include projects to strengthen human rights, political and civic participation, women's rights, religious tolerance, good governance, and anti-corruption efforts and to establish an independent media.

Democracy Promotion by U.S. NGOs

Non-governmental organizations dedicated to democracy promotion have been operating in Iraq since the fall of Baghdad in April 2003. Their activities include promoting civic participation in government, strengthening political parties, supporting the political participation of women, and promoting good governance.

These NGOs—including the National Endowment for Democracy and its major grantees: the National Democratic Institute for International Affairs (NDI), the International Republican Institute (IRI), and the Center for International Private Enterprise (CIPE)—work alongside Iraqi citizens to form and strengthen organizations that have become actively involved in Iraq's fledgling political process.

- The NDI and IRI host focus groups on a variety of political and public policy issues, facilitate regular meetings between Iraqi citizens and government officials, conduct national opinion polls, organize seminars to discuss the role of civil society organizations in a democracy, and arrange workshops to build the capacity of civic organizations to participate actively in the political process.

- CIPE concentrates on assisting Iraqi business leaders and other civil society groups in building a foundation for economic growth and democratic stability. Iraq's multitudinous political parties have received training in party organization, leadership, message development, voter outreach, communication, and media relations in an effort to build and strengthen political pluralism.

Upon arriving in Iraq, the NDI sought to reach out to as many Iraqis as possible. In addition to establishing a headquarters office in Baghdad outside the [Coalition-protected] Green Zone, it set up branch resource offices in Basrah, Hillah, Tikrit, Kirkuk, and Irbil. The branch offices were staffed by U.S. and Iraqi personnel and equipped with meeting rooms, libraries, and computer facilities, which were made accessible to local Iraqis interested in improving their respective communities. The branch offices served approximately 3,500 Iraqis each month. The NDI also helped to set up the lower house of the Iraqi legislature, the Council of Representatives, by providing technical assistance and support in helping legislators to learn their roles and responsibilities in a democratic body.

U.S. Government Efforts to Promote Democracy

U.S. government efforts to promote democracy, good governance, and individual rights are coordinated primarily through the U.S. Agency for International Development (USAID). For example, USAID initiated the Iraq Civil Society and Independent Media Program to support the establishment of an "informed, sustainable, and active Iraqi civil society" that will participate in Iraq's nascent democracy.

As part of its efforts, USAID established four regional Civil Society Resource Centers in Baghdad, Irbil, Hillah, and Basrah, which coordinate services for all 18 Iraqi governorates. The resource centers are staffed by personnel from America's Development Foundation (a U.S. nonprofit organization) and local Iraqis who provide training, technical assistance, and grants for developing Iraqi civil society organizations (CSOs). The resource centers have hosted over 1,100 training workshops to develop the core capabilities of the Iraqi CSOs.

The Iraqi CSOs stood up by USAID focus their efforts on several areas, including combating corruption, which was endemic under Saddam. To date, approximately 8,000 national, regional, and local government officials have been trained in an effort to promote transparency, accountability, fiscal responsibility, and other means of engendering governmental integrity. USAID and the Iraqi CSOs foster human rights by training Iraqis to monitor, report, and document human rights abuses.

Employment Will Aid Democracy

The benefits of increased employment and economic growth would give Iraqis greater hope for the future. It would lower hostility to both the Iraqi government and United States forces in Iraq. A prosperous and democratic Iraq could become a model for the Middle East, whose "silent majority" desperately wants to substitute greater political freedom and economic prosperity for religious radicalism and authoritarian rule.

Americans are right to be dissatisfied with the continued loss of American lives in Iraq and the tremendous burden Iraq places on our own economy. Pressing forward with a serious economic reconstruction program with our Arab allies providing the bulk of the funds offers hope for a more rapid transition to a democratic Iraq, increased political stability in the Middle East, as well as the homecoming of American troops.

Eric Davis,
"In Iraq, Democracy Is the Only Option,"
September 19, 2006. www.newhouse.com.

Helping Iraq Build Good Governance

Free and independent media have flourished in Iraq since the fall of Baghdad. USAID's Iraq Civil Society and Independent Media Program "is the only substantial supporter of in-country training, technical assistance, and funding" to Iraq's media sector. Through these efforts, USAID successfully established the first independent Iraqi news agency and the first independent public broadcasting service in the Arab world.

Under Saddam's highly centralized regime, Iraqis had no say in the national government and participated little in local governance issues. Community Action Programs (CAPs), a USAID grassroots effort, are aimed at alleviating that deficit. USAID works through several partners to manage reconstruction programs throughout Iraq.

The CAPs are intended to engage the Iraqi populace directly in planning and implementing rehabilitation and reconstruction projects in their own communities, thereby educating Iraqis in the fundamentals of democracy. These local rehabilitation projects "encourage communities to organize and elect inclusive and representative neighborhood councils" that then operate in a transparent and accountable manner to identify and prioritize community needs and to complete the projects. These grassroots efforts are critical to developing a capacity for local governance where it did not exist before.

USAID also operates in Iraq as part of multi-agency groups called Provincial Reconstruction Teams (PRTs). PRTs are relatively small operational units that are composed of U.S. diplomats, military officers, development policy specialists, and other stabilization experts. The military provides operational support and security for U.S. civilian personnel who work in PRTs, which are located in almost every province of Iraq.

The PRTs work with local Iraqi leaders to build local capacity in good governance, reconstruction, and economic development. Funding for reconstruction projects is provided through microloans and grants. Like the CAPs, the PRTs aim to train local Iraqi leaders in delivering essential services to their respective communities. To this end, the PRTs build relationships with local business and community leaders who desire to build a peaceful and democratic Iraq.

How a Withdrawal Would Scuttle Democracy Promotion

There are several dire predictions of what will happen in Iraq if the U.S. military withdraws. One possibility is that simmering sectarian violence would escalate into a full-scale Sunni-Shi'a civil war that would consume all of Iraq. Such an internecine civil war could topple the central government and its institutions and fragment the Iraqi armed forces. The steady stream of Iraqis leaving for Jordan, Egypt, and elsewhere could grow into a wholesale exodus. The resulting humanitarian crisis could lead to the deaths of hundreds of thousands of Iraqis. In the worst-case scenario, a Sunni-Shi'a civil war could spread beyond Iraq and become an international conflagration [conflict], engulfing Iraq's neighbors (and probably the U.S.) in a regional war.

The common thread of these predictions is that a U.S. troop withdrawal would lead to chaos throughout Iraq and that democracy, human rights, the rule of law, and individual freedoms would be among the first casualties. A complete breakdown of the Iraqi government would lead to anarchy and place Iraqi citizens in survival mode in which the safety and survival of their families would be more important than the advancement of democratic ideals.

> "The notion of quickly or ever trans-
> forming Middle Eastern countries into
> western democracies bespeaks at best a
> superficial appreciation of the peoples
> and the problems involved."

The United States Should Not Promote Democracy in Iraq

Terrell E. Arnold

In the following viewpoint, Terrell E. Arnold, a retired U.S. De-partment of State senior foreign service officer, argues that it is a folly to try to impose American-style democracy on Iraq. Accord-ing to Arnold, American democracy is corrupt and not a good model for a country of rigidly divided political, religious, and ethnic factions. More importantly, though, Arnold believes that political change in Iraq must come from Iraqis and must not be imposed upon them by foreigners.

As you read, consider the following questions:

1. How has America's agenda in Iraq changed over time, in Arnold's view?
2. Why does Arnold believe that majority rule would not work in Iraq?

Terrell E. Arnold, "The Fallacies of American Democracy for Iraq," Rense.com, Novem-ber 14, 2003. Reproduced by permission of the author.

3. Why does the author contend that a coalition withdrawal from Iraq could help the political situation in Iraq?

This week [November 2003] US [United States] civil administrator for Iraq, L. Paul (Jerry) Bremer, was called suddenly back to Washington for consultations on the obviously worsening security situation in Iraq. Bremer's return was accompanied by grumblings from the [George W.] Bush core team ([Secretary of State Colin] Powell, [Secretary of Defense Donald] Rumsfeld, [National Security Advisor Condoleeza] Rice, and the President) about the apparent ineffectiveness of the Iraqi Governing Council. Since the beginning of November more than forty American combat deaths have occurred; U.S. forces have lost three helicopters: American forces have gone to a warlike footing in the Sunni Triangle [northwest of Baghdad], and at least two direct attacks have been made on Bremer's headquarters. Meanwhile, the CIA predicts that the situation will get worse, an appraisal that Bremer is reported to share. It appears indeed time to review the bidding.

The Agenda for Iraq

One hopes that in this hastily called review, the situation and outlook for Iraq would be looked at squarely. Up to this point, the chances for that occurring, however, have appeared slim, because the administration, and by extension Bremer's team in country, has appeared fixated on carrying out the Bush scheme for transforming Iraq into an American style democracy. The habit up to now has been to look right by what US civil and military forces are doing in Iraq and to focus merely on how the Iraqis are reacting to the occupation and specifically on their growing resistance to the occupation. The answers to those questions are, of course, terribly important, but they will be useful only if they cause the US to review and modify its Iraq agenda.

On the face of things, the US agenda has changed several times already, from protecting the United States from a monster with weapons of mass destruction, to ridding Iraq of a brutal tyrant, to "liberating" the Iraqi people, and finally to creating a democracy in Iraq as the first stage in democratizing the entire region. This transition, perhaps better called a policy retreat, has convinced many governments and people that the US does not know what it is doing. The notion of quickly or ever transforming Middle Eastern countries into western democracies bespeaks at best a superficial appreciation of the peoples and the problems involved, but even worse, it reveals a severe lack of understanding of how our system actually is working these days.

The American Democratic Model Is Corrupt

American democracy today is in serious trouble. At the national level, the process of electing a president, or representatives and senators has become so expensive that only the wealthy or candidates supported by them can play. The process has been co-opted and corrupted by increasingly concentrated ownership of media and business, including banking, transportation, manufacturing, and energy. Legislative programs and goals largely focus on catering to the large organizations and the wealthy contributors. Our system was designed to work on a basis of majority rule, but effective control by a shrinking pool of elitists who also control both parties through contributions, has led to a situation in which not even the majority, albeit often invoked for political discussion, can decide any important issue.

In the meantime, majority rule has become an obsolete concept of governance in any complex society. Majority rule was a great step forward from absolute monarchy or despotism, but it is an inadequate concept for our time. Small but powerful groups have preempted the system. Consultations downward are weak and often superficial. Many minority and even majority interests are being pushed aside for benefits to elites. Therefore, what we are trying to export is really a theoretical concept that does not work in this country. How can we expect it to work in Iraq or elsewhere in the Middle East? Majority rule poses special problems in Iraq, and these have already been well identified. Since the majority of the people (around 60%) are Shiites, the fear of Sunnis, Kurds, Christians, Jews, as well as advocates of secular governance is that rule by majority, especially a fundamentalist one, would result in suppressing their interests and beliefs. Saddam Hussein sidestepped this problem by running a secular government, but he also played a preference game that made his Sunni compatriots (about 30% of the population) a de facto majority for governing purposes.

Bush's administration is behaving like a minority government with majority acquiescence. Conservative Christians, media and business elites, and the Israelis are setting the tone and calling the tune for a government that is systematically undoing generations of social legislation that was targeted on the American population at large. This approach, more than any other posture of the Bush administration, makes it clear that neither he nor his key team members understand or necessarily care to know what the problems of instability and conflict in the world are actually about.

Democracy Does Not Provide Government for All

The Bush argument is that "democratizing" Iraq will make the world a safer place. There is no evidence for this assertion. People who are left out of the political and economic mainstreams in countries such as the Philippines, Indonesia, Egypt, India, and numerous others are the principal sources of the world's terrorists. A system of governance that depends on the will of the majority that elected it, and therefore focuses pref-

Democracy May Bring the Intolerant to Power

The tide of public opinion today is not running in favor of pro-Western secular liberals, however, but rather the Islamists. In many Arab countries, this means that premature democratic elections will most definitely and predictably bring the mosque into the public square while driving out all other forms of expression. The tolerant are making democratic way for the intolerant, who in turn are very likely to block the possibility of any reverse flow of authority. How such dynamics promote liberal democracy in the longer run is hard to see. More likely, U.S. policies that foster pro-Islamist outcomes will delay political liberalization, help the wrong parties in the great debates ongoing in Muslim societies and, quite possibly therefore, make our terrorist problem worse.

Francis Fukuyama and Adam Garfinkle, "A Better Idea,"
Wall Street Journal, *March 27, 2006.*

erentially on the needs and wishes of that majority is exactly the troublemaker we already have. People who are not served by the system fight back however they can.

In our own system, key players have become totally preoccupied with the process. If you watch the President, you will readily see that his main business is to keep his party in power and to raise money for the next election. Since election, even in a time he avers is a crisis, he has spent easily a quarter of his time as President cultivating funding sources for elections, not only his own campaign but also for the campaigns of other Republicans. American taxpayers, of all political persuasions, paid the bill for this President to raise money for his re-election and for his own party by providing the best equipped airplane in the world, Air Force One, and the staffing infrastructure to support him, and of course paying his presidential salary while he is at the ranch raising money for the party. Other presidents have done this, but not as fulsomely as Bush.

The point here however is that our system at present is too occupied with the process of getting people elected, and not nearly enough with the business of running the country. The two are not one and the same, and no other country should copy this process, because it is fundamentally flawed in ways that make it incapable of providing government of all the people, by all the people and for all the people. Our system of governance grew up to meet the needs of an essentially white European society with differing religious and political views. Up until recently it appeared to be coping moderately well with the order of diversity the country now encompasses.

This discussion puts entirely aside the perverse notion of our insisting that the Iraqis or others must adopt our system of government. Democracy by fiat [decree] has never been the principle of our system. Forcing a system of government on another state is a peculiar application of the idea of popular governance.

Iraq Must Find Its Own Way

Iraqis in particular have experienced centuries of rule by outsiders from the arrival of the Osmanli, the Ottoman Turks, in the 16th century to the departure of the British in the 1950s. Iraqi nationalists threw out the British to form their own government only to discover all too soon that they were under the thumb of an indigenous tyrant. The Iraqi Governing Council is handicapped because it is tagged as a US tool. As such, it is unlikely to prosper unless it hands authority over to leaders chosen by the Iraqis. The longer that handover is delayed the more violence will occur, and the lesson of [2003 fighting] in Nasiriyah with the death of 17 Italian soldiers will be repeated. The CIA Station Chief in Baghdad appears to have delivered this message loud and clear.

The real message of the situation in Iraq is that broadly representative government, most likely chosen by traditional tribal and other community means, is the next vital step. The situation is simply too toxic to embrace an outside idea. Some new representative forms of governance are also needed to deal with Iraq's ethnically, educationally, religiously, and economically complex society. Ironically, the secularism introduced by Saddam had that potential and still does. But new forms or accommodations of each community's wishes must grow out of the traditions, customs, religions, felt needs, and preferences of the people seeking to be governed. The forms cannot be transplanted en masse or quickly.

There is no one size fits all, e.g., western democracy, solution to the problem. Thus there is no real solution the United States can provide other than early departure and a will—from outside—to help the Iraqi people find their own way. The argument against early American departure is that, if we leave, chaos will reign. With conditions as bad as they are, that is a hollow argument. Since outsiders and associated nationals are the main targets of much of the violence, things could actually calm down if the Coalition withdrew. In that event, perhaps the United Nations—with US and broad international support—could be persuaded to take on monitoring and development support functions, if those were acceptable to the Iraqi people.

Obviously the United States can and should promote representative government in the Middle East. But it is incapable of directly providing a workable model for Iraqi governance. The growing chaos shows clearly that US efforts to do so are unlikely to be accepted.

Periodical Bibliography

The following articles have been selected to supplement the diverse views presented in this chapter.

Spencer Ackerman   "In Iraq Forever," *American Prospect*, November 2007.

Brian Beutler   "Negotiating Our Future in Iraq," *American Prospect*, January 24, 2008.

Max Boot   "We Are Winning. We Haven't Won," *Weekly Standard*, February 4, 2008.

William Broyles   "Mission Impossible," *Texas Monthly*, July 2008.

Kevin Clarke   "Between Iraq and No Place," *U.S. Catholic*, August 2008.

Thomas Donnelly and Frederick W. Kagan   "We Still Need a Larger Army," *Wall Street Journal*, May 23, 2008.

Mohammed Fadhil   "The Mideast Won't Change from Within," *Wall Street Journal*, May 31, 2008.

Gian P. Gentile   "A (Slightly) Better War: A Narrative and Its Defects," *World Affairs*, Summer 2008.

Christopher Hayes   "End the War: Try Again," *Nation*, May 14, 2008.

Colin H. Kahl   "Walk Before Running," *Foreign Affairs*, July/August 2008.

Mark Kukis   "Should Iraq Prosecute U.S. Soldiers?" *Time*, August 26, 2008.

Terrence Samuel   "Winning the Peace," *American Prospect*, April 20, 2007.

CHAPTER 4

How Has War in Iraq Affected Terrorism?

Chapter Preface

Founded in 1988, the Islamic terrorist organization known as al-Qaeda has been held responsible for terrorist activities around the world, but their most notable attack came on September 11, 2001, when members of the organization hijacked airliners and crashed them into the World Trade Center and Pentagon in the United States. Part of the reason the United States and coalition forces invaded Iraq was to thwart Iraqi leader Saddam Hussein from harboring al-Qaeda and supplying terrorists with weapons of mass destruction that could be used in another catastrophic event like the September 11 attack.

Whether or not al-Qaeda and Saddam Hussein were connected is a moot point in the post-invasion world. What is more pressing is that an al-Qaeda affiliate in Iraq (originally known as Ansar al-Islam) is operating in the war-torn country, trying to strike at coalition targets and sow enough chaos to keep Iraq a battleground for as long as possible. In this way, al-Qaeda in Iraq (AQ-I—as the group is now referred to by the United States military) hopes to gather freedom fighters and earn respect from Muslim peoples who reject Western presence in the Middle East. According to a Congressional Research Service report from August 2008, "AQ-I has been a numerically small but operationally major component of the Sunni Arab-led insurgency that frustrated U.S. efforts to stabilize Iraq."

The *Weekly Standard* estimates that 90 percent of al-Qaeda in Iraq is composed of Iraqis, while the rest—including the majority of its leaders—are foreigners. Indeed, its current leader, known by the pseudonym Abu Ayyub al-Masri (Father of Hamza the Immigrant), is an Egyptian, who took the reins when his predecessor Abu Musab al-Zarqawi, a Jordanian, was killed in a U.S. airstrike in 2006.

As the 2006 pinpoint air attack on Zarqawi illustrates, the United States has hounded AQ-I until, as Pentagon officials claim, its operational effectiveness has declined significantly. Still, in 2006, al-Qaeda claimed responsibility for 60 percent of terrorist attacks in Iraq that year, but by May 2008, al-Qaeda attacks had fallen off by 90 percent. Many U.S. sources are now hesitant to link al-Qaeda with notable terrorist instances in Iraq, insisting that Washington may have overestimated the capabilities of AQ-I all along. Furthermore, because specific attacks blamed on al-Qaeda have resulted in the deaths of many Arabs—including Sunni Arabs, who were initially drawn to al-Qaeda—several tribes have turned their backs on al-Qaeda's cause and have even assisted coalition forces in hunting down operatives. Finally, the 2007 surge of U.S. troops in Iraq is thought to have helped seal AQ-I's fate.

In the following chapter, authors discuss the effect of U.S. operations and the occupation of Iraq on terrorist activities there and abroad.

| *"The war is breeding violent insurgent cells across the Arab world."*

War in Iraq Is Encouraging Terrorism

Joel Brinkley

In the viewpoint that follows, Joel Brinkley argues that the war in Iraq is breeding terrorism. In Brinkley's view, the amount of violence caused by Iraqi insurgents is increasing, and more worrisome, the U.S. occupation of Iraq is prompting many terrorists in the Arab world to take up arms against Middle Eastern governments friendly to the United States. Joel Brinkley is a professor of journalism at Stanford University and a former foreign policy correspondent for the New York Times.

As you read, consider the following questions:

1. What does Brinkley say accounts for the increased safety of Iraq in 2008 as compared to 2007?

2. According to Brinkley, what terrorist activities plagued Morocco in 2007?

3. What was Prince Saud al-Faisal's warning to the Bush administration in 2005, as Brinkley relates?

Y ou'll hear none of this from Washington, but the trends lines in Iraq are turning down again.

[In May 2008], the State Department published its annual report on terrorism around the world. And like most documents produced by the [George W.] Bush administration, it proved to be a misleading piece of propaganda. It said, for example, "There was a notable reduction in the number of security incidents throughout much of Iraq, including a decrease in civilian casualties" and "enemy attacks in the last quarter of the year."

Strictly speaking, that is true. But as Ambassador Dell Dailey, the State Department's counterterrorism coordinator, stood at the podium presenting this conclusion early [in May 2005], he was certainly aware that he was offering information that was four months out of date. I can't believe he didn't know that in the first months of 2008, the situation has reversed.

Death Toll Is Climbing

In [2008's] first quarter, the number of fatal bombings in Iraq spiked. Every month, ever-more American and Iraqi soldiers were being killed. For both, the number of deaths has doubled since December [2007]. Larger numbers of Iraqi civilians are dying, too.

These statistics come from the Iraq Index, a widely respected compilation of Iraq data published by the Brookings Institution. The numbers for April [2008] are incomplete but still suggest that the unfortunate trend is continuing. Consider the double suicide bombing of a wedding party in Diyala province [in May 2008]. It killed at least 35 people and wounded more than 60 others.

Even with the increase in violence, Iraq remains far safer than [in 2007], before President Bush's troop escalation. In the last few months, no foreigners have been kidnapped. No helicopters have been shot down.

America Must Withdraw from Iraq

If I believed in conspiracies, I would assume that George W. Bush was a jihadist plant, someone converted long ago to fundamentalist Islam and turned into a "sleeper" agent to be activated at the moment calculated to do America the most harm. That moment came obviously with Bush's election. His needless and heedless war in Iraq has done much to generate terrorism: created a living recruiting poster, spawned a variety of new terrorists, provided a national training ground, and placed tens of thousands of Americans within easy reach of ruthless killers. Osama bin Laden couldn't ask for much more.

But I'm not a conspiracy theorist, so I assume that a toxic mix of arrogance, ignorance, and incompetence is what caused the Bush administration to unintentionally give the terrorists so much help. Any policy of continued occupation in Iraq guarantees more terrorists and more terrorism around the world. If Americans want to defeat terrorism, America must withdraw from Iraq. Until the U.S. does so, the problem of terrorism will continue to worsen.

Doug Bandow,
"Fight Terrorism: Get Out of Iraq,"
April 27, 2007. www.antiwar.com.

Still, I found the State Department's latest Panglossian description of the war particularly egregious not just because the statistics were out of date. This report, the Bush administration's own assessment, painted a deeply troubling picture of the war's effect on the rest of the Middle East.

Encouraging Middle Eastern Terrorism

It showed that the war is breeding violent insurgent cells across the Arab world. Some of these insurgents intend to join the fight against the United States in Iraq. Other extremists, trained in Iraq, are taking up arms and recruiting suicide bombers to attack their own governments back home.

No one mentioned this during the long news conference about the terrorist report, and the document's authors made no effort to draw that conclusion from the disparate facts scattered about the 15,000-word chapter on the Middle East. But for anyone taking the time to read it, the conclusion was inescapable.

In Morocco [in 2007], "a series of suicide bombs shattered the relative lull in terrorist violence" over the previous five years, the report said. "Extremist veterans returning from Iraq" were training inexperienced insurgent fighters, who then carried out bloody attacks in Casablanca and other cities. King Mohamed VI observed that security in his corner of the Middle East is now "linked to the security of the region."

In neighboring Algeria, insurgents "used propaganda based on the call to fight in Iraq as a hook to recruit young people, many of whom never made it to Iraq but were redirected" to local insurgent cells instead. They carried out "high-profile terrorist attacks throughout the country."

Since 2003, insurgents have poured back and forth across Saudi Arabia's border with Iraq, and shortly after the war began, they started setting off massive bombs and killing foreigners at home.

Gen. Mansour al-Turki, Saudi Arabia's Interior Ministry spokesman, once told me that Saudi militants "wanted to spread their war against the United States and found that doing this was easier in their own country."

He drew this conclusion, he said, from interviews with insurgents he had arrested.

"The invasion of Iraq enabled them to convince others in the country to share their goals. For that reason, the invasion was very important to them."

No One Is Listening

The terror report described similar patterns in Jordan, Syria, Kuwait, Yemen and elsewhere. Still, asked in an NPR [National Public Radio] interview [in May 2008] whether the Iraq war is spawning insurgent violence in other countries, Dailey offered an astonishing answer that contradicted his own report. The war, he said, "has not spawned it at all."

In 2005, Prince Saud al-Faisal, the Saudi foreign minister, came to Washington to warn the Bush administration that the Iraq war threatened "to bring other countries in the region into the conflict."

"This is a very dangerous situation," he said. "A very threatening situation."

Then, as now, no one seemed interested in listening.

"Iraq is part of the war on terror again because the terrorists have chosen to make it so."

War in Iraq Is Necessary to Defeat Terrorism

David Limbaugh

In the following viewpoint, David Limbaugh argues that the war in Iraq is a central part of the U.S.-sponsored war on terror. Limbaugh claims the United States did not choose to make Iraq into a perpetual battleground; the terrorists who do not wish to see a democratic beacon in the Middle East have done so. Limbaugh lambastes liberals for rejecting the importance of the Iraq War and for calling for immediate U.S. troop withdrawal. David Limbaugh is a lawyer and political commentator whose writing has appeared in the Washington Times and several Internet news organs. He is also the author of Bankrupt: The Intellectual and Moral Bankruptcy of Today's Democratic Party.

As you read, consider the following questions:

1. In Limbaugh's view, how are liberals manipulating the leak of the April 2006 National Intelligence Estimate report to discredit the Bush administration?

David Limbaugh, "Handing Terrorists a Victory," TheVanguard.org, September 29, 2006. Reproduced by permission.

2. Why are Democrats unable to "contribute constructively" to the U.S. policy in Iraq, as Limbaugh claims?

3. When did "round 2" begin in the Iraq War, according to
Limbaugh?

The New York Times has again selectively leaked sensitive
national security information, this time cherry picking an
April [2006] National Intelligence Estimate (NIE) report to
support the left's template that our attack on Iraq has spawned
more terrorism. In response, President [George W.] Bush de-
classified other portions of the report to complete the picture.

If anything, on balance the report emphasizes how critical
Iraq is to our ultimate victory in the war on terror. But how
dare Bush defend himself?

Caught crying wolf again, Democrats have pulled a familiar trick out of their playbooks. They are demanding Bush de-
classify the entire document, knowing he cannot afford to
comply and reveal secrets to the enemy, to create the false im-
pression that he has something to hide. In the meantime, the
national interest be damned.

A Pernicious Pattern

Democrats pulled the same kind of stunt during Miguel
Estrada's Senate confirmation hearings for the appellate bench.
As one of their bogus excuses for filibustering Estrada seven
times, they said the White House was not forthcoming enough
about Estrada's record. So they demanded the release of intra-
office memoranda Estrada had written from 1992 to 1997 as
assistant solicitor general.

The White House properly refused to release the memos
because it would set a dangerous precedent and have a chill-
ing effect on the willingness of government counsel to give
frank advice. All seven living former solicitors general, three
having served under Democratic presidents, sent a letter to
Democratic Sen. Patrick Leahy to dissuade him from pursuing

Emboldening the Terrorists

Iraq is the convergence point for two of the greatest threats to America in this new century—al Qaeda and Iran. If we fail there, al Qaeda would claim a propaganda victory of colossal proportions, and they could gain safe havens in Iraq from which to attack the United States, our friends and our allies. Iran would work to fill the vacuum in Iraq, and our failure would embolden its radical leaders and fuel their ambitions to dominate the region. The Taliban in Afghanistan and al Qaeda in Pakistan would grow in confidence and boldness. And violent extremists around the world would draw the same dangerous lesson that they did from our retreats in Somalia and Vietnam. This would diminish our nation's standing in the world, and lead to massive humanitarian casualties, and increase the threat of another terrorist attack on our homeland.

George W. Bush, "President Bush Discusses Iraq,"
April 10, 2008. www.whitehouse.gov.

the memos. They said the memos were highly privileged and such an intrusion "would come at the cost of the Solicitor General's ability to defend vigorously the United States' litigation interests. . . ."

But this bipartisan plea didn't deter these partisan-intoxicated senators from their bad faith mission. They would do whatever it took to block this highly qualified, honorable nominee, even if it meant damaging the national interest. If you don't detect a pernicious pattern here, you're not looking hard enough.

Lack of Democratic Consensus on Iraq

Just like their witch hunt against Estrada, they have been trying to discredit President Bush's justifiable invasion of Iraq, which they supported at the time. I don't suppose we'll ever hear the end of this charge that our attack on Iraq has created more terrorists.

It's understandable that they insist on dwelling in the past since they are incapable of offering any alternative policy on Iraq. But what, finally, is the point of their relentless cacophony? How does it contribute, constructively, to our policy on Iraq?

Their obvious point is that we were not justified in attacking Iraq. Does that mean they believe we should withdraw now? Well, they just aren't sure, are they? They can't even build a consensus around that issue. So their only purpose in repeatedly leveling the charge is to discredit President Bush and score political points. You see, Democrats believe that if they can show—which they cannot—that our attack on Iraq set back our cause in the war on terror, President Bush and Republicans will be revealed as inept in conducting the war and safeguarding our national security.

Terrorists Have Made Iraq a Battleground

But the truth is that we were justified in attacking Iraq for a number of reasons, including that [former Iraqi leader] Saddam [Hussein's] Iraq was a terrorist-sponsoring state and thus a threat to the region, to us and to our allies. We ended Iraq's support of terrorism when we deposed Saddam.

That's when round 2 began, as insurgents and terrorists stepped in to reconvert Iraq to a terrorist haven. The terrorists are the ones who have made Iraq a terrorist battleground—not because they are mad that we attacked secular Saddam, but because they don't want a democratic beachhead in the Middle East, or a victory for the United States in the war on terror. They prosper in the shadows and die in the light of democracies and pluralistic societies.

If Democrats want to cling to the deluded belief that Saddam's Iraq was innocuous, not pursuing WMD [weapons of mass destruction], not violating U.N. and post-war treaties, not a threat to us and the region, let them dwell in the perverse nostalgia of their revised history.

Democrats can remain in denial, but Iraq is part of the war on terror again because the terrorists have chosen to make it so, just like they chose to attack us on 9/11 [2001]. The April NIE report makes clear that our victory in Iraq is essential to our victory in the war on terror. If you want to spawn more terrorism, try withdrawing precipitously from Iraq and see how that emboldens Al Qaeda's cause.

How can it reasonably be denied that Democrats are behaving as though they want to hand the terrorists their first major victory?

| "Where is the morality and legality in using an innocent country to serve as a 'war-on-terrorism' magnet?"

U.S. Occupation of Iraq Has Unjustly Turned the Nation into a Terrorist Magnet

Jacob G. Hornberger

In the following viewpoint, Jacob G. Hornberger asserts that part of the George W. Bush administration's rationale for fighting a war in Iraq is to make it a magnet for terrorism, thus ensuring that the terrorists will be occupied there and not conducting attacks in the United States. Hornberger questions what such a war has to do with terrorism—because the administration failed to show a link between Iraq and terrorists—and he is angered that Iraqi people are being forced to pay in blood for a war that has nothing to do with them. Jacob G. Hornberger is founder and president of the Future of Freedom Foundation, a public policy organization that promotes libertarian ideals.

As you read, consider the following questions:

1. What are the most important facts about the Iraq War that Hornberger says Americans must never forget?

Jacob G. Hornberger, "Is Bush's War on Terrorism in Iraq a War Crime?" *Future of Freedom Foundation*, November 21, 2005. Reproduced by permission of the publisher and author.

2. How does the author dismiss the rationale that the Iraq War is being fought for the liberation of the Iraqi people?

3. What does Hornberger believe is the ultimate solution to the wrongful invasion and occupation of Iraq?

After U.S. troops failed to find weapons of mass destruction (WMDs) in Iraq, which had been the [George W.] Bush administration's primary reason for invading Iraq, one of the president's alternative rationales for his war has been the so-called magnet rationale. It goes like this: Even though we failed to find WMDs in Iraq, we'll make Iraq the central front in the "war on terrorism" by making U.S. troops a "magnet" that will attract "the terrorists" to attack U.S. soldiers in Iraq rather than people in the United States.

But the magnet rationale raises an important question: Why is it moral to use an innocent country for such a purpose, especially when the targeted country is going to be thrown into chaos and destruction and tens of thousands of citizens of that country are going to be killed and maimed in the process?

We must never forget the most important facts about the Iraq War: Iraq never attacked the United States or even threatened to do so. Moreover, neither the Iraqi people nor their government participated in the 9/11 [2001] attacks. In this war, the United States was the aggressor nation.

The Bush Rationale for War in Iraq

President Bush's primary rationale for waging his war of aggression, a type of war punished by the Nuremberg War Crimes Tribunal, against Iraq was that Iraq's ruler, Saddam Hussein, not only possessed WMDs but also was about to attack the United States with them. Bush and other U.S. officials marketed the war by terrifying the American people into believing that Saddam was about to unleash nuclear, biological, or chemical weapons on American cities. Bush, Vice-President [Dick] Cheney, and other U.S. officials continually ridiculed UN [United Nations] inspections as incompetent and inadequate and constantly emphasized that Saddam Hussein was a liar when he denied possessing WMDs.

Soon after the invasion, when U.S. officials discovered that Saddam's denials regarding WMDs had been true, they had two options. One option was to apologize for their mistake and immediately exit the country. That was not the option they chose. Instead, they continued waging war, killing and maiming countless Iraqi soldiers who were continuing to resist an invasion that had been based on a false premise and thousands of Iraqi civilians as "collateral damage."

Permit me to digress once again to address the other alternative rationale that U.S. officials relied upon when the WMDs failed to materialize—that the invasion was mounted out of love and concern for the Iraqi people in order to liberate them from a dictator. All the circumstantial evidence leads to but one conclusion—that this alternative rationale is a lie. Recall the evidence: There was the Persian Gulf intervention, in which thousands of Iraqis were killed without any remorse on the part of U.S. officials. There was the Pentagon's intentional destruction of Iraqi's water and sewage facilities, knowing that infection and disease would spread among the Iraqi people. There were the brutal sanctions that contributed to the deaths of hundreds of thousands of Iraqi children. There was the U.S. government position that the deaths of those children were "worth it." There were the illegal no-fly zones in which more Iraqis were killed. And there were the torture, sex abuse, rape, and murder of Iraqis detained in U.S. prisons in Iraq, even after the fall of Saddam Hussein. I repeat: All the circumstantial evidence leads to an attitude of callous ruthlessness toward the Iraqi people on the part of U.S. officials, not love and concern for their freedom and welfare.

The Immorality of the Magnet Plan

Let us return to the magnet rationale—that it's better that U.S. troops fight "the terrorists" in Iraq rather than here in the United States.

But where is the morality and legality in using an innocent country to serve as a "war-on-terrorism" magnet, especially when the use of a country for that purpose generates even more terrorism? If there is a war between "the terrorists" and the U.S. government, why should the Iraqi people be made to pay the price for such a war? Why should their homeland be devastated, their people killed, their museums ransacked, their economy destroyed, and their entire nation thrown into chaos and conflict? What did they have to do with the war between the U.S. government and the "terrorists"? Why was it right to use their nation as a terrorism magnet—attracting violent insurgents and suicide bombers—and even taunt the terrorists to "bring it on"? Where is the morality in the deaths and maiming of tens of thousands of Iraqi people, both military and civilian, as part of a "war on terrorism" that was no business of the Iraqi people? Where is the legality, under U.S. law or international law, of using Iraq for such a purpose?

Since neither the Iraqi people nor their government ever attacked the United States or even threatened to do so—and since their ruler had complied with the UN's resolutions that required him to destroy his WMDs, they had a right to be left alone by the U.S. government. They had a right not to have their nation turned into a "magnet" for "the terrorists." They had a right to be left out of the U.S. government's "war on terrorism."

America Must End Its Aggression

No matter how brutal Saddam was, that was the business of the Iraqi people, not the business of the U.S. government, just as brutal dictators in Saudi Arabia, Egypt, Pakistan, Iran,

Syria, North Korea, China, Vietnam, Cuba, and Venezuela are the business of citizens of those countries, not the business of the U.S. government.

Some argue that the solution to all this is simply for U.S. troops to exit Iraq. That's not enough. The only genuine foreign policy solution is to dismantle the U.S. Empire, end the U.S. government's role as international policeman, interloper, and aggressor, and restore a constitutional republic to our land along with the peace, stability, prosperity, and harmony that would come with it.

> "These days, the Americans routinely fire missiles into Fallujah and other dense urban areas; they murder whole families."

Foreign Occupation of Iraq Is Terrorism

John Pilger

In the following viewpoint, John Pilger argues that the foreign occupation of Iraq is basically terrorism. Pilger claims that western governments and media entities have divided the world into terrorists and "us." This results in a distorted way of looking at events so that actions by terrorists are automatically evil and horrible, yet similar actions by "us" are necessary to defend freedom and democracy. John Pilger is an investigative journalist and documentary filmmaker who contributes to the New Statesman.

As you read, consider the following questions:

1. In May 2004, American forces killed how many people in Fallujah?

2. What historical event does Pilger relate to these killings in Fallujah?

John Pilger, "John Pilger Hears Blair Echo Mussolini," *New Statesman*, September 20, 2004. Reproduced by permission.

3. How many known cases are there of Iraqis dying at the hands of British soldiers? How many soldiers were charged?

The world is dividing into two hostile camps: Islam and "us". That is the unerring message from western governments, press, radio and television. For Islam, read terrorists. It is reminiscent of the cold war when the world was divided between "Reds" and us, and even a strategy of annihilation was permissible in our defence. We now know, or we ought to know, that so much of that was a charade; released official files make clear the Soviet threat was for public consumption only.

A One-Way Mirror

Every day now, as during the cold war, a one-way moral mirror is held up to us as a true reflection of events. The new threat is given impetus with each terrorist outrage, be it in Beslan or Jakarta. Seen in the one-way mirror, our leaders make grievous mistakes, but their good intentions are not in question. Tony Blair's "idealism" and "decency" are promoted by his accredited mainstream detractors, as the concocted Greek tragedy of his political demise opens on the media stage. Having taken part in the killing of as many as 37,000 Iraqi civilians, Blair's distractions, not his victims, are news: from his arcane "struggle" with his Tweedledee, Gordon Brown, to his damascene conversion to the perils of global warming. On the atrocity at Beslan, Blair is allowed to say, without irony or challenge, that "this international terrorism will not prevail". These are the same words spoken by Mussolini soon after he had bombed civilians in Abyssinia.

Heretics who look behind the one-way mirror and see the utter dishonesty of all this, who identify Blair and his collaborators as war criminals in the literal and legal sense and present evidence of his cynicism and immorality, are few; but they have wide support among the public, whose awareness has never been higher, in my experience. It is the public's passionate indifference, if not contempt, for the political games of Blair/Brown and their courts, and its accelerating interest in the way the world really is, that unnerves those with power.

Let's look at a few examples of the way the world is presented and the way it really is. The occupation of Iraq is presented as "a mess": a blundering, incompetent American military up against Islamic fanatics. In truth, the occupation is a systematic, murderous assault on a civilian population by a corrupt American officer class, given licence by its superiors in Washington. In May [2004], the US marines used battle tanks and helicopter gunships to attack the slums of Fallujah. They admitted killing 600 people, a figure far greater than the total number of civilians killed by the "insurgents" during the past year. The generals were candid; this futile slaughter was an act of revenge for the killing of three US mercenaries. Sixty years earlier, the SS Das Reich division killed 600 French civilians at Oradour-sur-Glane as revenge for the kidnapping of a German officer by the resistance. Is there a difference?

These days, the Americans routinely fire missiles into Fallujah and other dense urban areas; they murder whole families. If the word terrorism has any modern application, it is this *industrial* state terrorism. The British have a different style. There are more than 40 known cases of Iraqis having died at the hands of British soldiers; just one soldier has been charged. In the current issue of the NUJ magazine, *The Journalist*, Lee Gordon, a freelance reporter, wrote: "Working as a Brit in Iraq is hazardous, particularly in the south where our troops have a reputation (unreported at home) for brutality."

Neither is the growing disaffection among British troops reported at home. This is so worrying the Ministry of Defence that it has moved to placate the family of the 17-year-old soldier David McBride by taking him off the AWL list after he

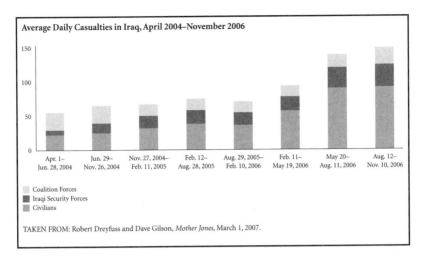

Average Daily Casualties in Iraq, April 2004–November 2006

Coalition Forces
Iraqi Security Forces
Civilians

TAKEN FROM: Robert Dreyfuss and Dave Gilson, *Mother Jones*, March 1, 2007.

refused to fight in Iraq. Almost all the families of soldiers killed in Iraq have denounced the occupation and Blair, all of which is unprecedented.

The Truth Is Suppressed

Only by recognising the terrorism of states is it possible to understand, and deal with, acts of terrorism by groups and individuals which, however horrific, are tiny by comparison. Moreover, their source is inevitably the official terrorism for which there is no media language. Thus, the state of Israel has been able to convince many outsiders that it is merely a victim of terrorism when, in fact, its own unrelenting, planned terrorism is the cause of the infamous retaliation by Palestinian suicide bombers. For all of Israel's perverse rage against the BBC—a successful form of intimidation—BBC reporters never report Israelis as terrorists: that term belongs exclusively to Palestinians imprisoned in their own land. It is not surprising, as a recent Glasgow University study concluded, that many television viewers in Britain believe that the Palestinians are the invaders and occupiers.

On 7 September [2004], Palestinian suicide bombers killed 16 Israelis in the town of Beersheba. Every television news report allowed the Israeli government spokesman to use this tragedy to justify the building of an apartheid wall—when the wall is pivotal to the causes of Palestinian violence. Almost every news report marked the end of a five-month period of "relative peace and calm" and "a lull in the violence". During those five months of relative peace and calm, almost 400 Palestinians were killed, 71 of them in assassinations. During the lull in the violence, more than 73 Palestinian children were killed. A 13-year-old was murdered with a bullet through the heart, a five-year-old was shot in her face as she walked arm in arm with her two-year-old sister. The body of Mazen Majid, aged 14, was riddled with 18 Israeli bullets as he and his family fled their bulldozed home.

None of this was reported in Britain as terrorism. Most of it was not reported at all. After all, this was a period of peace and calm, a lull in the violence. On 19 May [2004], Israeli tanks and helicopters fired on peaceful demonstrators, killing eight of them. This atrocity had a certain significance; the demonstration was part of a growing non-violent Palestinian movement, which has seen peaceful protest gatherings, often with prayers, along the apartheid wall. The rise of this Gandhian movement is barely noted in the outside world.

The truth about Chechnya is similarly suppressed. On 4 February 2000, Russian aircraft attacked the Chechen village of Katyr-Yurt. They used "vacuum bombs", which release petrol vapour and suck people's lungs out, and are banned under the Geneva Convention. The Russians bombed a convoy of survivors under a white flag. They murdered 363 men, women and children. It was one of countless, little-known acts of terrorism in Chechnya perpetrated by the Russian state, whose leader, Vladimir Putin, has the "complete solidarity" of Blair.

"Few of us," wrote the playwright Arthur Miller, "can easily surrender our belief that society must somehow make sense. The thought that the state has lost its mind and is punishing so many innocent people is intolerable. And so the evidence has to be internally denied."

It is time we stopped denying it.

Periodical Bibliography

The following articles have been selected to supplement the diverse views presented in this chapter.

Peter Bergen and
Paul Cruickshank

"The Iraq Effect: War Has Increased Terrorism Sevenfold Worldwide," *Mother Jones*, March 1, 2007. www.motherjones.com.

Max Boot

"Are We Winning the War on Terror?" *Commentary*, July/August 2008.

Current Events

"Five Years of War," March 10, 2008.

Warren Mass

"Did We Get Lied into War?" *New American*, July 7, 2008.

Mark Mazzetti

"Spy Agencies Say Iraq War Worsens Terrorism Threat," *New York Times*, September 24, 2006.

New York Times

"The Truth About the War," June 6, 2008.

Olivier Roy

"Al-Qaida Not a Threat When U.S. Leaves Iraq," *NPQ: New Perspectives Quarterly*, Spring 2008.

Jennifer Schuessler

"A History of Abuse in the War on Terror," *New York Times*, July 22, 2008.

Bret Stephens

"There Is a Military Solution to Terror," *Wall Street Journal*, June 3, 2008.

Jim Wallis

"Iraq: The Tipping Point," *Sojourners Magazine*, September/October 2007.

Fareed Zakaria

"The Only Thing We Have to Fear. . . ." *Newsweek*, June 2, 2008.

For Further Discussion

Chapter 1

1. What rhetorical strategies does President George W. Bush use to make a claim that the new Iraqi regime of Nouri al-Maliki is strong, representative, and unified? What evidence does Charles Krauthammer use to discredit al-Maliki's government? Whose argument do you find more convincing? In shaping your answer, point out how you would refute the other's argument.

2. Although many observers have praised the Iraqi police for their sacrifice and bravery in taking on a dangerous duty, the majority has criticized Iraqi units for being corrupt, ungoverned, and unprepared for the tasks at hand. Michael J. Totten is one of the few Americans to suggest that some Iraqi police units are reliable and willing to serve under difficult conditions. How does the unit that Totten visited compare to the ones described by Kevin Whitelaw? What might account for Totten's optimistic view?

3. According to C. Todd Lopez, what accounts for the coming readiness of the Iraqi army to defend the nation and take over more tasks assigned currently to coalition forces? What does Campbell Robertson claim the Iraqi army will require before it can assume more duties? Looking at the strengths and weaknesses that the two authors report, what role would you presently give to the Iraqi military units?

Chapter 2

1. Edward P. Joseph and Michael E. O'Hanlon contend, at the time the article was written, that Iraq should be parti-

tioned because of irresolvable sectarian conflicts. Reidar Visser, on the other hand, suggests that Iraqi's overwhelming sense of nationalism would never tolerate a partitioning. Gather some more viewpoints on partitioning and explain—using evidence from the authors in this chapter and others—whether you believe that partitioning would benefit Iraq. Also explain whether you think a partition of Iraq would be beneficial to U.S. interests.

2. Throughout the viewpoints in this chapter, critics of plans to partition Iraq claim that various problems, such as the following, would ensue if the nation was divided up into states: (1) discontentment over water and oil rights, (2) relocation of refugees, (3) greater conflict among Iraq's sects, (4) potential influence from neighboring powers, and (5) destruction of the national economy. Assume that the critics are right (or at least that those enacting partition would have to be sensitive to these claims) and rank these five issues from the most problematic to the least problematic. For each, explain why you have ranked them as you have.

Chapter 3

1. After reading the viewpoint by Ted Galen Carpenter and the two-part viewpoint by Erik Swabb and Mohammed Fadhil, decide whether you think the United States should keep troops in Iraq. Explain the advantages of your decision and ultimately project when you think U.S. troops should leave Iraq.

2. Terrell E. Arnold opposes the compulsory conversion of Iraq to American-style democracy because as he says, "Forcing a system of government on another state is a peculiar application of the idea of popular governance." Steven Groves, however, maintains that American institutions are helping the Iraqi people to strengthen civic participation, safeguard human rights, and create an indepen-

dent media. Do you think Groves's success stories are evidence of America forcing an agenda upon Iraq? Is there a way to reconcile Arnold's fears with Groves's hopes? Explain your answer.

Chapter 4

1. Read the viewpoints by Joel Brinkley and David Limbaugh. Decide which opinion you agree with and cite evidence from that viewpoint to explain why you support that view. Also cite counterevidence from the opposing viewpoint and explain why those arguments do not seem valid.

2. Jacob G. Hornberger asserts that the United States is waging war in Iraq, in part, to draw anti-American terrorists to that battlefield and thus keep them away from the American homeland. What evidence does Hornberger use to support his claim? In your opinion, is this argument sound? Explain why or why not. Additionally, address Hornberger's final contention—namely, that the business of overthrowing tyrants belongs to the citizens of those oppressed countries. Do you agree that the United States should never actively seek to free people enslaved by brutal regimes? Describe under what circumstances it may be permissible for America to become involved in the toppling of tyrannical governments.

Organizations to Contact

The editors have compiled the following list of organizations concerned with the issues debated in this book. The descriptions are derived from materials provided by the organizations. All have publications or information available for interested readers. The list was compiled on the date of publication of the present volume; the information provided here may change. Be aware that many organizations take several weeks or longer to respond to inquiries, so allow as much time as possible.

American Enterprise Institute (AEI)
1150 Seventeenth Street NW, Washington, DC   20036
(202) 862-5800 • Fax: (202) 862-7177
Web site: www.aei.org

Since its founding in 1943, the American Enterprise Institute (AEI) has worked to promote public policy that is in accordance with conservative ideals such as limited government, a strong national defense, and free market economics. The organization has generally supported the Bush Doctrine, which calls for a proactive national defense, and has supported the goals and mission of the Iraq War. Scholars at the institute call for continued U.S. involvement in the country until it is stabilized, and they are supportive of the current Iraqi government and leadership. The *American* is the monthly magazine of the AEI; articles from this publication and additional commentary and policy analysis are available on the organization's Web site.

Brookings Institution
1775 Massachusetts Avenue NW, Washington, DC   20036
(202) 797-6000
E-mail: communications@brookings.edu
Web site: www.brookings.edu

Based in Washington, D.C., the Brookings Institution seeks to provide accurate and thoughtful, independent research in order to construct policy recommendations which will make the American democracy stronger, guarantee that all Americans have social and economic security and opportunity, and ensure that the international system remains stable and open. Essays examining the current situation in Iraq, considering the positions of the Iraqi government as well as the policy options for the United States, can be accessed on the Brookings Web site. In addition, the Brookings Institution Press has published many books concerning Iraq and U.S. policy toward this country.

Carnegie Endowment for International Peace

1779 Massachusetts Avenue NW, Washington, DC   20036
(202) 483-7600 • Fax: (202) 483-1840
E-mail: info@carnegieendowment.org
Web site: www.carnegieendowment.org

The Carnegie Endowment for International Peace works to achieve increased cooperation between nations globally and encourages the United States to take an active role in the international community. The organization opposed the U.S. invasion of Iraq and has continued to analyze and monitor U.S. and Iraqi progress. Carnegie Endowment scholars have written extensively on U.S. options for continued engagement in Iraq and the possible results of U.S. policy decisions for both countries. *Foreign Policy* is the organization's bi-monthly magazine; articles from this publication, additional reports, and commentaries are available online.

Cato Institute

1000 Massachusetts Avenue NW, Washington, DC   20001
(202) 842-0200 • Fax: (202) 842-3490
Web site: www.cato.org

The Cato Institute is a libertarian think tank advocating limited government involvement in social and economic matters, and favoring a free market economy. The institute promotes a

U.S. foreign policy, which provides sufficient protection for the sovereignty of the country, but does not cross the line into interventionist and empire building. Cato has been critical of the George W. Bush administration's decision to begin a war in Iraq and argues that the United States should end its occupation of the country as soon as possible. Copies of Cato studies, reports, and commentaries concerning the current situation in Iraq can be accessed on the institute's Web site.

Center for American Progress (CAP)
1333 H Street NW, 10th Floor, Washington, DC   20005
(202) 682-1611 • Fax: (202) 682-1867
E-mail: progress@americanprogress.org
Web site: www.americanprogress.org

The Center for American Progress (CAP) seeks to promote a liberal and progressive agenda focused on ensuring that labor and civil rights are granted to all Americans. The Center believes that America should be an international leader to ensure peace and stability worldwide. With regard to the Iraq War, CAP believes that the United States should withdraw troops from Iraq and come to terms with the sectarian fissure of the country. Still, the organization advocates for continued involvement and dialogue between the United States and Iraq to foster peace and stability in the region. Reports on the current situation in Iraq can be found online.

Center for Strategic and International Studies (CSIS)
1800 K Street NW, Washington, DC
(202) 887-0200 • Fax: (202) 775-3199
Web site: www.csis.org

Experts at the Center for Strategic and International Studies (CSIS) research and analyze issues relating to defense and security policy, global problems, and regional studies in order to provide policy suggestions for individuals in government. Reports from the institute concerning Iraq include "The Ongoing Lessons of the Afghan and Iraq Wars," "Progress in Iraq: The December Report on Measuring Stability and Security in

Iraq," and "The Tenuous Case for Strategic Patience in Iraq," among others. The *Washington Journal* is the official publication of the institute.

Council on Foreign Relations (CFR)

Harold Pratt House, 58 East Sixty-Eighth Street
New York, NY 10065
(212) 434-9400 • Fax: (212) 434-9800
Web site: www.cfr.org

Council on Foreign Relations (CFR) is a nonpartisan, membership research organization that provides information on current foreign policy decisions and the process of foreign policy making. Educational materials are made available for both the public and policy makers in an attempt to foster informed debate and decision-making. While acknowledging recent advances made in Iraqi security, the CFR cautions against placing unrealistic expectations on the new Iraqi government and security forces, and is weary of a hasty withdrawal of U.S. forces. The bi-monthly publication of CFR is *Foreign Affairs*; the CFR Web site offers copies of articles from this magazine and additional publications such as backgrounders, op-eds, and transcripts of testimony.

Global Policy Forum (GPF)

777 UN Plaza, Suite 3D, New York, NY 10017
(212) 557-3161 • Fax: (212) 557-3165
E-mail: gpf@globalpolicy.org
Web site: www.globalpolicy.org

Global Policy Forum (GPF) serves as a watchdog over the United Nations to ensure accountability for decisions that impact the international society. Additionally, the organization seeks to mobilize citizens to act and ensure that their best interests are being met by the international community. GPF has a section of inquiry dedicated solely to the political, humanitarian, and historical issues relating to the Iraq conflict, examining the actions taken by the United States, and assessing the outcome of potential actions that may be taken in the future. All reports can be accessed at the GPF Web site.

GlobalSecurity.org

300 N. Washington Street, Alexandria, VA   22314
(703) 548-2700 • Fax: (703) 548-2424
E-mail: info@globalsecurity.org
Web site: www.globalsecurity.org

GlobalSecurity.org serves as an Internet clearinghouse of information on all security related topics, from the military to homeland security. The Web site contains a searchable database of articles as well as a section providing up-to-date publications on Iraq. Freely downloadable white papers covering security topics and a list of security related magazines offering free subscriptions can be found at www.globalsecurity.org.

Heritage Foundation

214 Massachusetts Avenue NE, Washington, DC   20002-4999
(202) 546-4400 • Fax: (202) 546-8328
E-mail: info@heritage.org
Web site: www.heritage.org

As a conservative public policy institute, the Heritage Foundation is dedicated to the promotion of policies consistent with the ideas of free enterprise, limited government, individual freedom, traditional American values, and a strong national defense. The Heritage Foundation has been supportive of the Iraq War and overthrow of Saddam Hussein from the first days of the invasion. The foundation also supports continued occupation of that country until its government has achieved an acceptable level of stability and control, so that it can serve as a U.S. ally in the region against other powers such as Iran and Syria in the fight against terrorism and Islamic extremism. Publications outlining the organization's stance on the Iraq War can be read on its Web site.

Middle East Policy Council (MEPC)

1730 M Street NW, Suite 512, Washington, DC   20036
E-mail: info@mepc.org
Web site: www.mepc.org

The Middle East Policy Council (MEPC) conducts political analysis of issues relating specifically to the Middle East and encourages ongoing debate through its conferences for educators and government officials. The council is uniquely situated in its ability to analyze the current situation in Iraq due to its expertise on the region. Articles assessing the war in Iraq and what must be done to stabilize the country can be accessed on the MEPC Web site. The quarterly journal *Middle East Policy* serves as the organization's official publication.

Peace Action
1100 Wayne Avenue, Suite 1020, Silver Spring, MD   20910
(301) 565-4050 • Fax: (301) 565-0850
Web site: www.peace-action.org

Peace Action is a grassroots organization advocating for non-violent government policy, utilizing write-in and Internet campaigns in combination with citizen lobbying to put pressure on elected officials. The organization believes that pre-emptive war is not a foreign policy option and opposed the invasion of Iraq. Peace Action calls for the United States to withdraw military forces from Iraq and believes that the military actions taken by the United States against Iraq have decreased national security. The Peace Action Web site provides reports by the organization, along with information about how to become involved in current projects.

Progressive Policy Institute (PPI)
600 Pennsylvania Avenue SE, Suite 400
Washington, DC   20003
(202) 547-0001 • Fax: (202) 544-5014
Web site: www.ppionline.org

Progressive Policy Institute (PPI) offers a progressive perspective on how government policy should serve the citizens of the United States, moving away from traditional views and the left-right debate. PPI believes that global stability can be achieved through the promotion of economic and political freedom. The institute insists that the positive strides made so far in Iraq must be acknowledged, even while admitting that the war was a mistake, and that methods such as opening up free trade avenues with Muslim countries will do more to help win the war on terror than fighting alone. On its Web site, subscriptions to periodic e-newsletters, press releases, op-eds, and other PPI publications are available.

U.S. Department of Defense (DoD)

1400 Defense Pentagon, Washington, DC   20301-1400
(703) 428-0711
Web site: www.defenselink.mil

The U.S. Department of Defense (DoD) is the branch of the United States government charged with protecting the country by utilizing and leading all branches of the U.S. military. They are the people on the ground in Iraq and charged with securing the country through the use of military techniques. Updates on progress in the Iraq War can be read on the DoD Web site.

Washington Institute for Near East Policy

1828 L Street NW, Suite 1050, Washington, DC   20036
(202) 452-0650 • Fax: (202) 223-5364
Web site: www.washingtoninstitute.org

The Washington Institute for Near East Policy seeks to promote an increased understanding of the relationship between the United States and the Middle East as a region. Additionally, it advocates for a continued involvement between the two to ensure peace and stability in the region. The institute has examined the impact of the Iraq War on all ethnic and religious groups in the region and has also conducted research into how U.S. policy toward the war will impact the country in the future. Reports expanding on these issues are available on the organization's Web site.

Bibliography of Books

Ali A. Allawi   *The Occupation of Iraq: Winning the War, Losing the Peace.* New Haven, CT: Yale University Press, 2007.

Daniel Byman   *The Five Front War: The Better Way to Fight Global Jihad.* Hoboken, NJ: John Wiley & Sons, 2008.

Zaki Chehab   *Inside the Resistance: The Iraqi Insurgency and the Future of the Middle East.* New York: Nation, 2005.

Patrick Cockburn   *Muqtada: Muqtada al-Sadr, the Shia Revival, and the Struggle for Iraq.* New York: Scribner, 2008.

Toby Dodge   *Inventing Iraq: The Failure of Nation-Building and a History Denied.* New York: Columbia University Press, 2003.

Gwynne Dyer   *After Iraq: Anarchy and Renewal in the Middle East.* New York: Thomas Dunne, 2008.

Douglas J. Feith   *War and Decision: Inside the Pentagon at the Dawn of the War on Terrorism.* New York: HarperCollins, 2008.

Noah Feldman   *What We Owe Iraq: War and the Ethics of Nation Building.* Princeton, NJ: Princeton University Press, 2004.

Charles Ferguson   *No End in Sight: Iraq's Descent into Chaos.* New York: Public Affairs, 2008.

Peter Galbraith — *The End of Iraq: How American Incompetence Created a War Without End*. New York: Simon & Schuster, 2006.

Lloyd C. Gardner and Marilyn B. Young — *Iraq and the Lessons of Vietnam, or How Not to Learn from the Past*. New York: New Press, 2007.

Michael M. Gunter — *The Kurds Ascending: The Evolving Solution to the Kurdish Problem in Iraq and Turkey*. New York: Palgrave Macmillan, 2008.

Ahmed Hashim — *Insurgency and Counter-Insurgency in Iraq*. Ithaca, NY: Cornell University Press, 2006.

Joost R. Hiltermann — *A Poisonous Affair: America, Iraq, and the Gassing of Halabja*. New York: Cambridge University Press, 2007.

Radha Iyengar — *Is There an "Emboldenment" Effect?: Evidence from the Insurgency in Iraq*. Cambridge, MA: National Bureau of Economic Research, 2008.

Seth G. Jones — *How Terrorist Groups End: Lessons for Countering Al Qa'ida*. Santa Monica, CA: Rand, 2008.

Charles W. Kegley Jr. and Gregory A. Raymond — *After Iraq: The Imperiled American Imperium*. New York: Oxford University Press, 2007.

David Kinsella — *Regime Change: Origins, Execution, and the Aftermath of the Iraq War*. Belmont, CA: Thomson/Wadsworth, 2007.

Quil Lawrence	*Invisible Nation: How the Kurds' Quest for Statehood Is Shaping Iraq and the Middle East.* New York: Walker & Company, 2008.
Wojtek Mackiewicz Wolfe	*Winning the War of Words: Selling the War on Terror from Afghanistan to Iraq.* Westport, CT: Praeger Security International, 2008.
Thomas Mowle, ed.	*Hope Is Not a Plan: The War in Iraq from Inside the Green Zone.* Westport, CT: Praeger Security International, 2007.
Yitzhak Nakash	*Reaching For Power: The Shi'a in the Modern Arab World.* Princeton, NJ: Princeton University Press, 2006.
Yitzhak Nakash	*The Shi'is of Iraq.* Princeton, NJ: Princeton University Press, 2003.
Loretta Napoleoni	*Insurgent Iraq: Al Zarqawi and the New Generation.* New York: Seven Stories, 2005.
Vali Nasr	*The Shia Revival: How Conflicts Within Islam Will Shape the Future.* New York: W.W. Norton, 2006.
Michael B. Oren	*Power, Faith, and Fantasy: America in the Middle East, 1776 to the Present.* New York: W.W. Norton, 2007.
George Packer	*The Assassins' Gate: America in Iraq.* New York: Farrar, Straus, and Giroux, 2005.

Norman Podhoretz — *World War IV: The Long Struggle Against Islamofascism.* New York: Doubleday, 2007.

William Roe Polk — *Understanding Iraq: The Whole Sweep of Iraqi History, from Genghis Khan's Mongols to the Ottoman Turks to the British Mandate to the American Occupation.* New York: HarperCollins, 2005.

Michael Scheuer — *Marching Toward Hell: America and Islam After Iraq.* New York: Free Press, 2008.

Steven N. Simon — *After the Surge: The Case for U.S. Military Disengagement from Iraq.* New York: Council on Foreign Relations, 2007.

Donald M. Snow — *What After Iraq?* New York: Pearson/Longman, 2009.

Jonathan Steele — *Defeat: Why They Lost Iraq.* New York: I.B. Tauris, 2008.

Joseph E. Stiglitz — *The Three Trillion Dollar War: The True Cost of the Iraq Conflict.* New York: W.W. Norton, 2008.

Reidar Visser and Gareth Stansfield, eds. — *An Iraq of Its Regions: Cornerstones of a Federal Democracy?* New York: Columbia University Press, 2008.

Kerim Yildiz — *The Kurds in Iraq: The Past, Present and Future.* London: Kurdish Human Rights Project, 2007.

Index